GOD'S GRACE
and
MAN'S HOPE

*An Interpretation of the
Christian Life in History*

Harper ≣ ChapelBooks

GOD'S GRACE
and
MAN'S HOPE

An Interpretation of the
Christian Life in History

BY

DANIEL DAY WILLIAMS

Harper ▲ ChapelBooks

Harper & Row, Publishers, New York

To

EULALIA WESTBERG WILLIAMS

"... we in our appointed work imployd
Have finisht happie in our mutual help
And mutual love ..."

THE RAUSCHENBUSCH LECTURESHIP FOUNDATION
OF THE COLGATE-ROCHESTER DIVINITY SCHOOL,
ROCHESTER, NEW YORK

The Rauschenbusch Foundation was established in March, 1929, at the Colgate-Rochester Divinity School in memory of the late Walter Rauschenbusch, illustrious exponent of social Christianity and, from 1902 to 1918, professor of church history in the Rochester Theological Seminary, to which institution the Colgate-Rochester Divinity School is successor.

The movement for the establishment of this foundation was initiated by a gift of ten thousand dollars from Mrs. Edmund Lyon, of Rochester, New York, conditioned upon the raising of twenty-five thousand dollars from other sources. An amount somewhat in excess of that sum was secured through the generous gifts of citizens of Rochester, alumni of the Rochester Theological Seminary, and others.

The general field of the lectureship is that of Christianity in its social expression and application. A series of lectures upon this foundation is to be given annually during the week of the Spring Convocation at the Colgate-Rochester Divinity School, these lectures to be published in book form and known as the Rauschenbusch Lectures.

CONTENTS

CONTENTS

PREFACE TO THE CHAPELBOOK EDITION

IN THE years since 1949 when this book was first published, the great paradox has grown even more sharp of a world in which man has increasing control over the conditions of life, yet at the same time stands under the ominous threat of his being dehumanized, if not destroyed, by the technological powers which he has unleashed. I believe, therefore, that the issues dealt with in the book are as crucial as ever, and I could hope that the argument here for a Christian faith and practice which does not shy away from the problems of technological society and political reconstruction is relevant to our needs in this era of world ferment and revolution.

New theological developments in these mid nineteen-sixties show three primary emphases. First, there is a call for concern with the secular and an insistence that the real issues between God and his people are to be met in worldly life and not primarily, if at all, in religious form. I have tried to show in this book that the work of God in the world involves what Whitehead has called God's "secular functions," and I am seeking the foundations for a theology which recognizes the ultimate significance of the secular without denying the importance of religious experience. Man's sense of the holy has not been eliminated from his life, and it is now as always one of the most powerful factors in human behavior.

A second major emphasis today is upon a contextual ethic of response to situations rather than application of principles. My aim in this book is an interpretation of the freedom of the Christian man to respond to the personal demands of life and history without being bound by a straight jacket of abstract principles; but I have also argued for the proper function of principles as guides to responsibility, and I maintain that a right understanding of the legitimate role of moral and legal principles is necessary for a valid ethic and for the political order.

A third trend in theology, one which has been reinforced by the analytic movement in philosophy, is the disdain for metaphysics. In some cases there is a turning to an existentialist personalist doctrine of being in which the classic quest for the rational structure of being is rejected. Here I cheerfully acknowledge that I stand against this tendency and regard it as an exaggerated and in many ways misplaced revolt against the element of metaphysical structure in all human thinking, an element which always reappears in new forms when it is repressed. I have here argued that the metaphysical doctrines of process philosophy, derived primarily from Alfred North Whitehead, can give us the flexibility and dynamic personalism we need, and still keep us at the task of seeking to grasp the intelligible aspects of a world in which things are significantly related to one another and in which God is the *logos* of being.

It seems to me that the writings of Dr. Reinhold Niebuhr since his Gifford lectures have become more explicit in their affirmation of the doctrine of an immanent growth of good and an element of common grace in God's working in history. I would like to think that the positions held in my book stand even closer now to Dr. Niebuhr's thought than they did a few years ago.

And of course in 1949 we were still ten years away from the call of Pope John XXIII for the Second Vatican Ecumenical Council. My book contains some criticisms of traditional Roman Catholic positions on theological and ethical questions. It is now clear that the Roman Catholic Church is undergoing a profound reexamination of its positions on many issues. As a Protestant I welcome this historic movement, and I look forward to deeper mutual learning and understanding among all the communions of Christendom. I have added a brief footnote to the notes to chapter six to indicate where the discussion would now take a new turn in relation to the Roman Catholic position.

For the rest, except for a few sentences altered for style or timeliness, I have let the book stand as originally published. I express my gratitude both to those who have encouraged me in its support and those who have given substantial criticisms through the years.

D.D.W.

Union Theological Seminary,
New York City
March 15, 1965

PREFACE

BELIEF that a good society is possible on earth has been one of the powerful constructive forces in the life of modern man. Today when it is necessary to human survival itself that the nerve of hope for that better society be kept alive, there is widespread bewilderment and anxiety. Have we, in spite of all idealism, succeeded only in preparing our doom?

I have written this book to state and defend two convictions about that hope. The first is that there is solid ground in human experience for believing that the better world can be made. It is cynicism and nihilism which in the last resort are unrealistic about what human life can be. The second conviction is that any enduring hope must be based, not upon man alone, but upon the fact that God is present in human history, and is there creatively and redemptively at work. To try to establish the City of Man on anything other than faith in God is to build on quicksand. These two convictions, taken together, place my thought within the tradition of the Christian social gospel of which Walter Rauschenbusch was both prophet and pioneer. It is an honor indeed to have the lectures which are here set down and expanded bear his name.

There is widespread agreement, in which I share, that the social gospel was too optimistic about man and his progress. There is also a growing impression that the "neo-orthodox" reaction to the liberalism of the social gospel is too pessimistic. I concur in this judgment also. But the point is not to add a little more optimism to balance so much pessimism. The point is to find that truer Christian understanding of man and God which can be expressed in a structurally sound theology. We need an interpretation of the Christian faith which can guide moral effort and sustain the exercise

13

of social intelligence while it strengthens our hold upon the reality of God's judgment and His mercy. Whether this book offers any basis for such a theology is for the reader to decide, but that is what I am after.

The way through the tangled issues which surround our theme leads to the discussion of many problems, the chief of which are: the nature of God's working and our knowledge of Him; the conflict between Christian love and power politics; the mystery of time and its relation to the idea of human progress; the meaning of the Christian's "calling" in the making of moral choices; the question whether there is a Christian ideal for society, and how such an ideal is to be stated; and finally the query which searches the human heart, whether and how it is possible for a man to love his neighbor as himself.

In seeking to give a reason for the Christian hope for man I have dealt critically with the work of several contemporary theologians from each of whom I have learned much. I have given special attention to the thought of Reinhold Niebuhr, and I hope that the attempt to state an alternative to his position on many points does not obscure my debt to him. His teaching, writing, and political action have been for me, as for so many, a major aid to Christian thinking in our time.

The list of all those who have contributed to my thought is too long to give here. I do want to acknowledge with gratitude the continuing encouragement and stimulating criticism of Dr. Justin Wroe Nixon. It is a pleasure to recall the gracious hospitality and the thoughtful attention given by President Edwin McNeill Poteat and the faculty, students, and alumni of Colgate-Rochester Divinity School, when the lectures were given at Easter time in 1947. For so many of the ideas which have lighted my theological way I am indebted to my teachers and colleagues, Wilhelm Pauck and Henry Nelson Wieman. On specific points James Luther Adams and Herbert W. Schneider made helpful criticisms. My father and brothers have patiently tried to let me in on the lawyers' under-standing of the law. For the positions taken, I am alone responsible. Mr. Hartley Ray did excellent detective work in locating elusive references. Mrs. Ruth Murphy prepared the manuscript with a skill and devotion beyond the call of duty. My wife, to whom the book is dedicated, not only typed the original lectures, but has shared with me throughout her intuitive theological wisdom for which no plodding reflection can ever be a substitute.

I have tried to show that God can use evil and error to serve good and truth. If through any truth it may possess, or any discus-sion of its shortcomings the book may contribute to the develop-ment in the Church of a more powerful witness to the Good News which our world so deeply needs, I am content.

D.D.W.

Chicago
New Year's Day, 1949

CHAPTER ONE

Two Theories of Man's Destiny

THE Christian religion has always created hope in the human spirit. It has produced men who live in the world of affairs with a unique expectancy. Christians see present wrong and failure as always surrendering the last word. New life, new good, new resource are forever available as God lives. In the concentration camps and battlefields and political struggles of our day the Christian faith has its witness in men and women whose separate hopes have been shattered and yet whose hope has never been taken away.

This book has been written out of the conviction that Christianity can bring to the human spirit today a rebirth of hope. It can enable us to face without fear or hysteria the grim struggle to bring the destructive powers now in our hands under some kind of intelligent control. It can help to set free the resources of will and intelligence which must be summoned if we are to achieve some tolerable solution of pressing human problems.

The further conviction which underlies this book is that there is an intellectual problem to be solved if the Christian faith is to possess that inner clarity which releases the power of Christian preaching and living. The particular problem to which the book is addressed is our confusion about the hopes by which we have been living. We Christians who believe in progress had such bright hopes for the world. And now we are perplexed about them. We share the anxiety and uncertainty of a world in which the optimistic idealism of the recent past appears naïve. When President Roose-

velt in his Fourth Inaugural Address said, "We shall strive for
perfection. We shall not achieve it immediately, but we shall
strive," even his slight qualification of optimism gave warning of
a radical shift toward a realistic temper.[1] Whatever realism there
has been in the spirit of democracy, and there has been a great deal,
it has generally had superimposed upon it a vision of perfection,
and with a notion of man's life as continually moving toward a
higher and higher good. Liberal Christianity shared that vision,
sometimes qualifying it with a more realistic appraisal of human
nature, sometimes exaggerating its romantic hopes. Today we
cannot imagine the recovery of that simple optimism nor have we,
most of us, any interest in returning to it. We know we must shift
from one perspective on human history to another. But to what?

The need is imperative for a restatement of the Christian doctrine
of man and his historical destiny. We must see the problem of
human progress from a Christian interpretation, recognizing that
it is not so simple a problem as romantic idealism made it, nor
yet so simple as the present somewhat contemptuous rejections of
it suggest. We must try to find a more compelling expression of the
Christian conviction that faith and hope and love are the abiding
realities which sustain the human spirit within and beyond the fates
of individuals and civilizations.

We shall get our bearings by setting forth in this first chapter the
two different ways in which Protestant thought today describes our
human pilgrimage and defines the kind of hope which is possible
for those who believe that God is, and that he has made himself
known to us in Jesus Christ.

I

Two sharply conflicting versions of the Christian faith about
man's life in history are competing for the mind of Protestantism
today. I shall use the terms "liberalism" and "neo-orthodoxy" as

labels for these two standpoints; but it should be understood that these terms are meant neither for praise nor for abuse; and further that each of them embraces many theological tendencies which need to be carefully distinguished. Still, in their broad outlines, these two interpretations of the course of the human pilgrimage and its outcome can be characterized and contrasted.

Both these theologies are Christian. They both attempt to solve the problems which have troubled Christianity from the beginning about the relation of God's final rule, His Kingdom, to the kingdoms of this world. In order to see clearly what the issues are let us begin by briefly recalling the bedrock convictions on which all Christian thought is raised as superstructure.

The foundation of all Christian faith is the conviction that the meaning of man's life lies in his relationship to God. When Milton's archangel Michael begins his prophetic story of the future of mankind his preface is: "Good with bad expect to hear, supernal grace contending with sinfulness of Man."[2] Here are the essentials of all Christian experience: man, the creature, standing between good and evil, sharing in both; man, the sinner, rebelling in his freedom against his Creator and Judge; God the merciful Father, contending for man's soul.

In the Christian faith all human history is understood as the working out of God's redemption of a world which He has created good, which has fallen away from Him, and which He redeems from sin and death through a victory whose cost is the death of His son on the cross. From the creation of the world before time to the consummation of all things at the end of time, the Bible describes the life of man with God as a series of events which taken together constitute the history of the work of redemption. The fall of Adam and Eve, the covenants with Israel and its deliverance from bondage, its falling away and punishment through new sufferings, the speaking of the divine word through the prophets, the birth of Christ in human flesh, the life and death of Jesus, the experience of the resurrection, and the history of the Church, the expectation of the final events and the established reign of God in love and peace— all this is the Biblical understanding of what God has done, is doing, and will continue to do for the judgment and redemption of the world. The Christian lives by the faith that this life comes forth from the hand of a good God, and by the assurance that its outcome is the victory of that goodness. This victory has a tragic side. The way is dark with suffering, sacrifice, and the death of God's son for our sakes. Redemption lies on the other side of judgment, and there are lost men who make their beds in hell. Yet against the darkness, the mercy of God shines clearly. The damned show God's justice, the saved show His mercy, and both show His glory. As "the stream of divine Providence" began in God, so it ends in God. "God is the infinite ocean into which it empties itself." Thus Jonathan Edwards characterized the meaning of the great drama.[3]

Alongside this triumphant faith there has existed from the beginning a perplexity in Christian thought. What is the relation between God's final victory, and the resolution of the immediate problems of justice, order, and peace in this world of time, death, and conflict? Does this redemption promise a new historical period when mankind shall have been restored to moral health and sanity? Are God and man together to "raise an Eden in this vast wilderness?" Why do the wicked prosper, and shall they always prosper, so long as man is man?

The greatest of the prophets of Israel wrestled with this problem and never resolved it. They pled for moral regeneration, calling upon the whole nation to turn its back on evil. Some of them, like Isaiah, made specific political suggestions as to Israel's responsibility before God. Yet the prophets were driven close to despair concerning the possibility of this rebirth. Perhaps only a remnant shall remain upon whom God can depend. Perhaps not even a remnant. Suppose God finds not even one righteous on the earth? As Israel moved through the violence and terror of the years approaching the birth of Jesus the hope for a Davidic King and a perfected state yielded to the vision of an apocalyptic shattering of this world in the final clash of God's power with the power of Satan. For that day men can prepare and watch as they live in this world which lies under the shadow of evil.[4]

For a brief moment the early Christian Church was able to overcome the uncertainty about the time of the conquest of evil. The Messiah had come, had been crucified, and was risen from the dead. He was coming again soon. It was enough to live in the little colony of his people, drawn apart from the corrupt world, seeking to save individuals and experiencing already that perfect love and joy which was the foretaste of life in God's Kingdom. When the Christ did not return and the Christians began to find their way in a world in which men still work and buy and sell and govern and go to war and die, the long story of the Christian attempt to be in the world and yet not of it had begun.

One can easily become cynical over the ensuing compromises with "the world," the accommodation of the Church to nearly every evil which has raged through human society, the plain perversity of this all too obviously human institution. But let us remember what the problem has been. Men who live with faith in the God of love continue to live in this world with its evil, and with this human freedom subject to every temptation. It is as if the Christian were holding before his eyes a map of eternity and trying to find his way along the broken paths of time. Two different countries! No wonder there has been stumbling, confusion, and a continuous argument along the way.

It is dangerous to make any one generalization about the multiplicity of ways in which Christians have tried to solve this problem; but this at least can be said. On the one hand, Christianity has never been willing to accept an irresponsible position either for the Church as institution or for the individual in relation to the problems of human society. It has maintained a continuous moral pressure against the evils which it has regarded as blocking the fulfillment of human life. On the other hand, there is a bewildering variety of ways in which Christians have interpreted the meaning of moral action, and the kind of expectations for man's life in history which it involves. Those who live by faith in God who is lord over all time can never quite be "domesticated" in this world. The conviction that we seek no earthly city here below, we seek a city to come, is at once the glory and the perplexity of Christian living. What then shall we do in the earthly cities?

We proceed now to examine the contrasting ways in which "liberalism" and "neo-orthodoxy" interpret the faith that the kingdoms of this world are judged by and are to become the Kingdom of God and of His Christ, and how they answer the problems which arise for the Christian when he seeks to express his faith in moral decisions.

II

By "liberal theology" I mean the movement in modern Protestantism which during the nineteenth century tried to bring Christian thought into organic unity with the evolutionary world view, the movements for social reconstruction, and the expectations of "a better world" which dominated the general mind. It is that form of Christian faith in which a prophetic-progressive philosophy of history culminates in the expectation of the coming of the Kingdom of God on earth. Its classic American expression is still, I believe, Walter Rauschenbusch's *A Theology for the Social Gospel*, which appeared at the time of America's entry into World War I.[5]

The liberal vision sees God working in human history for a progressive achievement of a higher order of life for mankind. The culmination of His work will be the establishment of a universal brotherhood of justice and love. The historical process taken in its overall course is thus essentially, if not wholly, the story of God's success with man. In the liberal perspective, we understand the meaning of our human existence when we see our place in this mighty drama of God's creative achievement.

Through infinite time God has been at work to make a world, and to make it a good world. With patience and power beyond our imagination He has made a cosmos out of primordial chaos. He moved through the struggle and surge of the evolutionary process, bringing new levels of life into being, and crowned His work with the creation of mind and spirit. He has created free men who can participate with Him in the ongoing task of world-making. Man has risen from savagery and barbarism to civilization in response to the divine working within him. In the progress of reason, in all cultural expression, and supremely in the growth of moral and religious insight man has had his life opened to the new adventure of partnership with God. God's power and purpose have been revealed everywhere; but it is in the experience of one people, the Hebrews, that the depth of that purpose was clarified and made known with power. In one life, which arose in the midst of that people, God uttered His truth and spirit in such a way that His love, which is His very essence, became known and operative in human history with transforming power. Through the light and spiritual life which stream from Jesus, mankind received the impulse which enables it to move upward toward the fulfillment of that unity of all life in love which is the Kingdom of God. The hope of the Christian rose to a crescendo during the bright days at the turn of the last century when it looked as if the ramparts of evil were beginning to be battered down. There is not a single barrier, men thought, lying across the creative advance of the great community of love which cannot be overcome. As one liberal thinker, Ozora Davis, expressed it,

> At length there dawns the glorious day
> By prophets long foretold;
> . . . .
> The day of dawning brotherhood
> Breaks on our eager eyes,
> And human hatreds flee before
> The radiant eastern skies.[6]

Only superficial thinkers who did not really understand this view of human life ever talked of the way upward as if it were easy. It is costly to God and to man. Only in the light of the sacrificial death of Jesus and the continuing sacrifice of all loyal servants of God can we see how really difficult is the way to His Kingdom. But the hope which lives in this faith is not shattered; for God does win His victory, gradually, as men are persuaded to respond to Him and to work with Him. This is His world and who can say that He cannot bring His Kingdom on earth? Does God will anything less than that His reign should be complete over all his creation?

This was no humanistic view. Man can do nothing without God. No one said this more clearly than did Walter Rauschenbusch: "The Kingdom is for each of us the supreme task and the supreme gift of God. By accepting it as a task, we experience it as a gift."[7] God works against the inertia of nature, the stupidity of men, self-ishness, cruelty, the wrong entrenched in institutions; so man should work against these with hope.

Given such a hope, the ethical task of the Christian is clearly one of loyal co-operation with God in world-making and world-fulfilling. To serve the God of love means to do what needs to be done to clear the way for that society of justice, peace, and growing brotherhood which God wills. It is true the liberal ethic split into two camps over the question of the means and strategy of this conquest. One group believed that the spirit of love is itself a pure and unique method for dealing with all evil; hence the Christian ethic is one which expresses this spirit persuasively, intelligently, in all situations, and withdraws from all methods and means which resort to something which is other than the spirit of love. Hence liberal Christian pacifism. Other liberals said that love must be expressed directly in all social struggles, but with the effective means at hand, whether political, economic, or even military which may be necessary in an imperfect world. On this ground nonpacifist liberals supported the nation in World War I.

In spite of differences on the ethical problem all Christian liberals conceived of ethical social action as rooted in a religious conception of the meaning of that action and with a religious faith which gives hope for its success. *It is in this union of the sacred and the secular that the real prophetic power of liberal Christianity is to be found.* It said to everyone, "When you do your best in the spirit of love to cope with the demands of God's justice and love in the political, social, and economic orders, indeed anywhere in life, there you are actually meeting God Himself, whose work is being done through you, and God is winning." Death comes to all; but for the most part the liberal faith conceived of immortality as a continuing opportunity for further growth and work with God.[8]

Thus to bring the inner realm of man's freedom and the whole outward task of human culture and social advance into one religious unity, with a clear ethical imperative and sustaining hope, was the supreme achievement of the liberal Christian mind. Its critics rarely appreciate its depth, its power, and its contribution to Christian thought. The prophetic element in the theologies which today criticize liberalism most vehemently are in part dependent upon the liberal achievement.

The word "progress" has been omitted from this interpretation of the liberal hope. The reason is that the secular doctrines of progress lack religious depth. Christian liberals used the term "progress"; but they never accepted the humanist's notion that progress can be achieved without God; nor did they accept the idea that progress is automatic. The religious understanding of the conflict between good and evil, the fact of the stubborn resistance of the human heart to the love of God and its demands, the vision of the divine strategy of sacrificial love in the life and death of Jesus as the climax of history, all this is foreign to most of the philosophies of progress, but it was the heart of the great expressions of Christian liberalism. It is true that the romantic vision of progress was seductive and many Christians succumbed to it. But one has only to read the book of a leading liberal, Dr. Harry Emerson Fosdick's *Christianity and Progress,* written in 1922, to see that the deeper insight of Christian faith was not surrendered. He said:

This is no foolproof universe, automatically progressive, . . . moral evil is still the central problem of mankind. . . . Jesus said that two masters sought man's allegiance, one God, the other mammon. . . . That conflict still is pivotal in human history. The idea of progress can defeat itself no more surely than by getting itself so believed that men expect automatic social advance apart from the conquest of personal and social sin.[9]

No progress "apart from the conquest of personal and social sin." Now over twenty-five years after Dr. Fosdick's remarkable book, we are even more deeply troubled about this conquest. What it is that makes us uncertain about the liberal faith is epitomized in a brief comment which appeared as the conclusion of a column written by the New York *Times* military expert, Hanson W. Baldwin, during the early days of February, 1945, when the struggle of the Nazis and the Russians was moving toward its climax. Baldwin wrote:

History has again turned full cycle. Teuton and Slav are locked again in the age-old tragedy of man, and the great death-grapple on Germany's eastern marches has begun. . . . For the surging tides of opposition, national and racial ambitions ages old, are meeting in ultimate conflict at the Oder and tide-rips and cross-currents will sweep across our world for generations to come.[10]

In these arresting lines a military analyst puts the stark reality which every philosophy of history must face. Here are the gigantic historical forces sweeping mankind along beyond the power of any individual or group to alter. Are we not as individuals embedded like bits of rock in the glacial forces of historical process? Here is the tragic clash of ambitions, hatreds, and ideals, for war is impossible without the enlistment of the pride, the loyalty, the ideals of men. Here is the undeniable truth that the consequences of this violent struggle will in large part form the shape of the world for centuries. We start with no clean slate in history; we start with what is left to us of both the achievements and the wreckage of the past. Here is the reminder of death, which puts a question mark after every human hope. Suppose now that war is not an isolated problem, but symptomatic of the whole plight of man. Suppose that there lies within human life everywhere an ineradicable conflict of powers and wills. What have faith and hope and love to do with human history if this be its substance and its outcome? "Neo-orthodox" theology has tried to answer that question.

III

"Neo-orthodoxy" is a term which points to that widespread movement in contemporary Protestant theology which seeks to recover the central theme of the Reformation: justification by faith in the redemption wrought by God in Jesus Christ, as the foundation of the Christian Gospel and of the Church. The three names which probably stand out most prominently when we think of this movement are Karl Barth, Emil Brunner, and Reinhold Niebuhr, not only because they are among its leaders, but because their writings are most widely known. Certainly there are important differences in method and in content among them. Some of these differences we must note later on. Here, however, I shall run the risk of treating the standpoint as a whole. My thesis is that all the neo-orthodox thinkers neglect a fundamental Christian insight into the meaning of life within the grace of God. They overlook it in different ways, but they all overlook it. The following characterization of the general tendency of neo-orthodoxy, including the thought of these three theologians mentioned, is, I believe, accurate.[11]

We must bear in mind one important way in which neo-orthodoxy differs in its view of history from traditional orthodoxy. The fall of man is no longer taken as an event at the beginning of human history, nor is the "end of history" a literal conception of a point of time at which the world ceases to be. All of this becomes "myth" or symbolic expression by which we can interpret the realities of our human situation.

Neo-orthodox theology sees human existence in the tragic perspective. The plight of man is this: man is so created in the very structure of his being that the meaning of his life is the realization of his freedom in love to God and to his neighbor. But man actually misuses this freedom, turns against God, his neighbor, and himself, making of his life a dark arena of anguish and greedy scramble. Now all Christian theology has said man is a sinner. But neo-orthodoxy is unique in this, that it returns to the doctrine of sin as the actual status of all men universally, but no longer depends upon an original "fall" of man for the explanation of the universality of sin. Sin is not a series of misdeeds from which we can be extricated through moral education and effort; it is a status which characterizes our human existence. Yet we are free beings who are actually sinners in our own self-will. Every man is his own Adam.

How can this universal actuality of sin against God in whose image we are created be understood? Neo-orthodox theologians say this is one of the places where reason breaks down. We can "understand" this only in faith. The fact is that we are sinners, everywhere, at all times. We can no more explain it than we can explain our existence itself.

It is one of the great merits of Reinhold Niebuhr's thought that while he regards the doctrine of "original sin" as a myth which is absurd to reason and necessary to faith, he has given us one of the most astute analyses of the source of sin in human nature which Christian thought has ever achieved.[12] His account is this. We are finite creatures, having our lives in the flux, the insecurity, the mystery of nature, of history, and of freedom. Finiteness is not sin. But free and finite creatures become anxious in the face of the perplexities and insecurities of life. Anxiety is temptation to sin, that is, to take flight from the self, or to the pride in which we seek to make ourselves more secure than we have a right to be. Anxiety is the serpent in the garden of life, and the serpent is always there. This leads to a most important consequence. If we want to understand sin, let us look first not at what we ordinarily call the badness of human nature; but let us look at the "goodness" of our ideals and moralities. For it is just at the point where we use our ideals, our reason, and our religion to baptize our special privilege, to rationalize our selfish interest, that sin is manifest in its most terrible and destructive form.

We must recognize now that we are not analyzing a temporary phase of the human situation; we are analyzing that situation as it necessarily is and must be so long as man is creature. Man will always be suspended between ideal perfection and the insecurities and imperfections of life. The temptation to sin is not eradicated by the development of man in history; for while we may eliminate certain insecurities, we cannot eliminate insecurity itself or the basic anxiety of human existence. Now we see why the Kingdom of God is a symbol for an order which stands beyond this existential order. The Kingdom can come only at the "end."

What, then, of hope for a better world? Here Niebuhr, Brunner, and Barth share the same general position, though with some differences in emphasis.[13] They all agree that the social orders which form the structure of human history, such as the family, the state, the economic order, betray an essential separation of man from God. The state, for example, must defend its order and its existence, establish a relative justice, restrain violence, by the use of the sword. So Karl Barth says: "The State as State knows nothing of the Spirit, nothing of love, nothing of forgiveness. The State bears the sword, and at the best, as seen in Romans XIII, it does not wield it in vain."[14] Economic activity is governed by calculations of profit, reward, and competition, not by principles of unselfish service. Even the family, where the direct expression of love between persons is possible, depends upon the compulsions of our sexual nature and the protections of custom and law for its order and stability.

Gunther Dehn puts the position extremely, "We must learn to recognize that there is no one form of State life, of economics, or of any other social order, that is more in the Spirit of the Gospel than another!"[15]

This view that the structure of our human life is both protection against our sinful nature, and at the same time opportunity for the manifestation of sin, has serious consequences for our expectations regarding the course of history. The inner contradictions of human life will again and again erupt in historical crises, wars, catastrophes, ages of despair in which the fact that life contradicts the demand of God's Kingdom will be disclosed. This is a tragic view of human history set over against a progressive view. History is education, but it is an education in humility. "Age after age the tragic empires rise."[16] Of course there are all kinds of developments in techniques and in cultural achievements; but the point is that man's moral position before God remains the same. Niebuhr says: "There is not a single bit of evidence to prove that good triumphs over evil in this constant development of history."[17] More recently he declares that man's plight becomes progressively worse: "The real fact is that while history solves many problems, it aggravates rather than mitigates the basic incongruities of human existence."[18] In support of this he points out that the development of greater scientific power also makes it possible for those with power to try to achieve a wider and more tyrannical dominion over larger areas of life.

The principle that Christian ethics and the Christian hope are correlative is illustrated by this doctrine of man's predicament in history. Neo-orthodoxy holds that what the liberal expected, the transformation of the orders of this world into social orders which express and support the expression of Christian love, is precisely what we cannot hope for. What we must understand about the orders is that they are what they are because we do not love God and our neighbor as we ought. Even the reborn man in whom the spirit of love has become the new way of life still lives in a world which contradicts that love, and the conflict is never resolved in this life, even within his own soul.

The question of what we can and ought to do in a world which does not yield directly to love is the most difficult problem that this theology has to face. The answers given to it vary considerably. In Brunner's *The Divine Imperative*, and in Reinhold Niebuhr's writings we have been given profound analyses of the moral problem. There is something for the Christian to do. There are elements of justice, of freedom, even of brotherhood to be achieved through human effort in society. We must do what we can in response to the love of God, yet as those who know that the world in which we act will be, until the end of time, in opposition to that love. We can appreciate the Christian absolutist who seeks to stand wholly against involvement in the evil of society; yet as he does so he must realize that those who are working for relative gains within the social order are doing a necessary work in the service of God.

Whatever one thinks of this theology, it wholly misses the mark to interpret it as an ethical retreat. It looks like retreat to liberals because it denies certain notions by which liberalism supported social action. But ours is a world of concentration camps and atomic bombs, and the omnipresent threat of war. In such a world the neo-orthodox theologians have set ringing again the great bell of evangelical faith. They have asserted faith in God and in the necessity of moral effort before the very doors of hell. They see that Paul's words are addressed as much to our time as to his: "The whole creation groaneth and travaileth in pain together until now; . . . and even now we groan within ourselves waiting for our adoption, to wit, the redemption of our bodies, for we are saved by hope."[19]

We have reviewed, then, two ways in which the Christian mind has tried to grasp the infinite mystery of the human pilgrimage. Both are Christian; both have their roots in the prophetic moral thrust of the Gospel against the wickedness of human society and the human heart; both believe that Christian responsibility leads us to act in the political and social order for the sake of human justice and decency; both rest our human hope finally upon God's saving power and His promises.

The controversy between these theological standpoints has been instructive, and it must go on. But the thesis which I wish to state and defend in this book is this: *as contemporary Protestant Christians we are not forced to make a simple choice between liberalism and neo-orthodoxy.* The conviction has been growing among many that we cannot make such a choice, partly because there is truth on both sides, but especially because *both* have left something out which is the very basis of all Christian experience. That is the fact of redemption. Theologically speaking what is wrong with both schools is that they have no place for God's *redemptive* work in human history. Liberalism has no place for redemption because it does not see the need for it. It conceived the emergence of man from sin and the overcoming of evil as primarily a problem of creation, the making of the new man and the new world. Neo-orthodoxy recognizes the need for redemption; but it has never made an adequate place for the real possibility of redemption as transformation of our human existence, hence it postpones redemption to another realm. These statements may be too sweeping, but I believe they are essentially just. Neither liberalism nor neo-orthodoxy has fully interpreted the fact that we know God both as Creator and Redeemer. Let us see where this clue to theological reconstruction leads.

IV

Christian theology has always held that God the Creator in making His world makes it a good world. It has held that there is real evil in this world and in man which must be overcome. But it has also said that God actually moves with power and wisdom and love in our human history to redeem the world from its evil, and man from his sin. In the prophets, in Jesus Christ, in the continuing life of the Church, and in all of life, God the Redeemer makes available to us resources which are our defense against the despair which comes when evil lays waste to life. Take Paul's words out of the New Testament and out of Christian experience and what have we left of Christian hope—"and may the Lord make you increase and excel in love to one another and to all men . . . so as to strengthen your hearts and make them blameless in holiness."[20] What we need is a theology which will hold together the fact of the creation of the good world, the fact that evil invades that goodness, and the fact of a redemption which brings hope in the midst of tragic failure and loss.

Christian theology should hold the doctrine of the new life created by the redemptive love of God as the center of its interpretation of Christian experience. Such a theology would continue in the succession of those who have affirmed the experience of the new life in Christ. It would have a close relationship to the pietism of the Protestant sects, to Wesley and Edwards; but it must be far more realistic in its understanding of the continuing limitations of the life of the Christian than former theologies have been. The way to theological reconstruction lies through the attempt to discover why both liberalism and neo-orthodoxy have failed to emphasize the reality of the redeemed life. If we can point out the errors which cause this failure we can go on to show that there is a theology which squares more adequately with what we know in Christian experience.

In the chapters which follow we shall be engaged in this criticism of both liberal and neo-orthodox presuppositions in the attempt to establish an alternative theological foundation. It will help to guide us through the argument if we list here briefly the major presuppositions of the two schools which stand in the way of their achieving an adequate doctrine of redemption.

Liberal theology has always tended to obscure the nature of sin; hence it has never adequately expressed the depth of our dependence on the redemptive work of God. The reason for this is to be found not only in the liberal emphasis upon the goodness of God. It is also in the fact that the cause of sin was often attributed to factors for which man cannot be held responsible and thus sin was explained away.

1. Sin was sometimes ascribed to inheritance of animal instincts. Professor Case, for example, in his *The Christian Philosophy of History*, suggests that a beastly strain "inherited from Neanderthal man" is responsible for the terrible cruelties in our contemporary civilization.[21] The readiness with which liberals accepted explanations of human wrongdoing in terms of some specific unfortunate circumstance in the history of the race or of the individual is somewhat puzzling, as Reinhold Niebuhr has shown. It surely detracts from man's spiritual stature as a free moral agent, to suggest that every misuse of his freedom is caused by something outside himself. The explanation is that liberals found it hard to believe that man would willfully misuse his freedom. Further, the doctrine that evil has its source in specifiable maladjustments or difficulties inherited from the past supported the belief that these causes could be removed, and the belief that the course of evolutionary development would progressively leave the sources of difficulty far enough behind so that their influence would be nullified.

2. When either our animal or our primeval ancestors were not given the responsibility for our plight the blame was shifted to the social institutions which corrupt human nature. What happens here in liberalism is another case of a truth being pushed beyond its proper limits. Of course men are corrupted by evil social institutions; but if the social processes fully explain man's behavior, then the freedom which liberalism has claimed for man is denied.

So Mr. Garnett:

Human nature is on the side of human progress. The problem is to set aside the *damnosa hereditas* of prejudice, false tradition, superstition, fear, hatred, that survives from the childhood of the race, and to develop institutions adequate to its maturity. There is in the human heart enough of natural good will. It remains for intelligence to enable it to find its way.[22]

3. Finally, and in some contradiction to the first two positions, liberals asserted that man in his own freedom can do what needs to be done to throw off the evil forces which corrupt him. Mr. F. Ernest Johnson, for example, in his admirable re-examination of the social gospel, speaks of the sins of contemporary men, and then says, "let them purge themselves of whatever demonic pride they have been guilty of."[23] But can man purge himself of demonic pride? Is not the very assumption that he can do so a reinforcement to that pride? It is the man who can confidently say to himself, "I have purged myself of demonry," for whom further self-understanding is impossible. Man can repent only if he knows that the righteousness of God is always in part a judgment against him.

Neo-orthodoxy has recovered for us a profound analysis of the reality of sin and the need of redemption. But it has not made clear how redemption actually makes any difference in this life in this world. For Karl Barth man always appears to remain on the knife edge between the love of God and the abyss of damnation.[24] Reinhold Niebuhr holds that we are redeemed from sin in principle, but whether we are redeemed in fact is not made clear.[25] Christ, he says, is our hope, not our possession.[26] And again he suggests that only in the moment of prayer can man really love God and his neighbor with the love which Christ has shown to us.[27] Emil Brunner comes closer to positive affirmation of the new life of the man to whom the love of God has come with power. Yet Brunner describes the new nature as "consisting in the struggle against the old nature," and what is accomplished in the struggle is not clear.[28] I have spoken in broad terms of these three representatives of this school. I believe that in whatever way the new life of faith, or in faith, is admitted as an actual reality by them, it exists alongside of a continuation of the actuality of sin in such a way that the new life is always just sheer beginning or sheer hope. It never is described as a perceptible and orderly movement toward a new structure for this human existence.

There are three reasons why no convincing assertion of a real "growth in grace" appears in this school:

1. Neo-orthodoxy's treatment of the doctrine of original sin has led to a distorted version of the natural life of man. Dr. Niebuhr, for example, holds that the created order is good, yet it produces such insecurity that man is so tempted that sin is inevitable. Where now is the goodness of the creation? It is further clear that Niebuhr regards as evil many aspects of life which are not necessarily evil. He holds, for example, that all conflict within the self or between selves is evil. But one has only to think of play, or of the element of growth in conflict, or of the educative value of coercion to realize that conflict is not necessarily evil. The friction of mind against mind, will against will, is part of the natural stuff of human life. It is the way in which we become human. In Brunner a similar distortion appears in his doctrine that all the orders of existence defeat *agape* in so far as they are impersonal. It is only as an accommodation to sinful man that the impersonal structures, which for Brunner include all the rational and legal elements in the orders of creation and of culture, exist. But, we ask, are not impersonal privacy, the element of impersonality in law, and the impartiality of ethical principle necessary to the growth of persons in community? Brunner's commitment to the doctrine that *agape* can exist only in the relationship of "I and Thou" in which all impersonal elements are eliminated is based upon an erroneous conception of human nature. That error always appears in Christian theology when the doctrine of original sin is not very carefully stated. I propose to examine this error and to show that in Niebuhr and Brunner's thought there is

an inverted romanticism in which all the natural conditions of human existence are erroneously regarded as barriers to the Kingdom of God.

2. In the second place, neo-orthodoxy has its own metaphysics in which time and process are dealt with in such a way that the element of connected development in Christian experience must be denied. Neo-orthodoxy has accepted the doctrine that human freedom exists in a series of "moments" which involve only eternity on God's side and the "decision" on ours. This notion is inherited from Kierkegaard. In Kierkegaard's philosophy there is no redemptive activity of God as a process in history, nor can there be, for there is no real becoming in the realm of freedom. All the meaning of existence collapses into the existential moment. It is not accidental to his view but implied in it, that the individual's relations to his fellows is of minor significance. The isolated individual stands alone before God, others offer only the occasion, or so to speak, the stage setting for the moral and religious act. This is also why Kierkegaard has no real place for the Church in his theology. I do not deny in the least the significance of the dimension of individual freedom in God and the importance of Kierkegaard's recovery of it. But it is a distortion of the Christian experience to neglect the factor of social process, in which the cumulative historical consequence of the work of freedom is given its place. Chapter Five is addressed to this problem.

3. Neo-orthodox theology emphasizes the true insight that the redeemed man is never beyond the need for redemption. All progress in holiness brings with it new temptation. But we get no sufficient doctrine of the Christian life by pointing out only what man cannot become. We need also to say what can be achieved by God's power in human action. Niebuhr is right in saying that there is no solution of the problem of redemption in terms of the formulas of pietism. The word "sanctification" has not acquired its peculiar odor for nothing. The saint who is proud even of his humility is too common

a phenomenon in Christian history. Yet either some break with sin in fact as well as in principle is possible or else the whole of Christian experience is a delusion. That break takes place in human experience, in history, in the process of life.

The clue to the reconstruction of Protestant Christian faith in our time is to recall to ourselves the fact that *God, the Lord of life, is both Creator and Redeemer.*

We shall consider now what the foundations of a Christian interpretation of human destiny would be from this standpoint.

CHAPTER TWO

God: The Creator and Redeemer

Two Christian versions of the course of human history were sketched in broad strokes in the first chapter. Both these interpretations fail, we argued, to do justice to the Christian experience of redemption. There is a work of God which makes possible a new life in which the disorder, sin, and tragedy of our existence are borne in faith, and begin to be overcome. Therefore we must consider a third version of the way of God with man. It involves the assertion of the real possibility of a new life which is born out of the encounter of the sinner with God's mercy. It involves another conception of the meaning of the tragic course of human history. Here a new ground for hope, the only ground, as I believe, for ultimate hope, is found.

Our problem is to give an account of man's life when seen from the viewpoint of the Christian experience of redemption. But every theological assertion raises the question of the basis on which it is made. This is the problem of evidence, of the tests of truth. We must make clear the conception of Christian truth which underlies our argument. It should be said that my main concern in this book is not with theological method but with one issue in Christian theology, namely, how we are to interpret the Gospel hope of redemption. Such a problem can be discussed fruitfully within the Christian Church, using the Christian words, and referring to the common body of Christian experience, even among those who may differ on the problem of the tests of Christian truth. It has been truly said, for example, that no one can read Reinhold Niebuhr's Gifford Lectures without coming to know himself better because of Niebuhr's profound insight into human nature. This holds whether or not one agrees with Niebuhr's theological method at all points. Yet it is true that the problem of truth is involved in all fundamental discussion. I shall be as explicit as possible about the presuppositions concerning how we know what we know, and the general philosophical ideas in relation to which this interpretation of the Christian faith is developed.

I

This reference just made to philosophical presuppositions identifies our thought with one type of Christian theology and cuts across the dominant tendency in the neo-orthodox movement, where philosophy is wholly rejected by theology as in Barth, or is given a merely peripheral role as in Brunner, and, to a lesser extent, in Richard Niebuhr and Reinhold Niebuhr. It may contribute to clarity if I make here the flat statement that I believe all Christian theology without exception involves general ideas about the world, and about man. These ideas are drawn from our human experience, and when given a critical analysis and elaborated, they are philosophical concepts. Such terms as "world," "eternal," "good," and indeed, "guilt," "sin," "God," are not the exclusive possession of the Christian vocabulary. The ideas for which they stand bring Christian theology into organic relation with all human experience. It can be shown that beginning with the Bible itself, down through the theology of Luther to that of Barth general philosophical ideas have entered into the substance and structure of the Christian mind. Luther cannot be understood without Occam, Brunner cannot be understood without Kierkegaard, Barth cannot be understood without Kant! This is not to say that philosophy drawn from general human experience controls theology. Christian experience is unique. It has its own integrity and its distinctive source of insight in a particular historical experience. Concepts like guilt and conversion do not mean the same thing in Christian speech as they do in Hindu mysticism or in a clinic for psychoanalysis. Christian thought need never be subservient to or identified with some particular philosophical doctrine or system. But Christian thought can never be expressed without making use of the general concepts which it is the business of philosophy to clarify and criticize. Theologians ought to be as self-conscious as possible concerning the philosophical presuppositions which they use as they interpret the Christian faith. If this is not done these presuppositions are not eliminated. They remain hidden and uncriticized.[1]

Two general notions are presupposed in all that follows in our interpretation of redemption. The first involves the conception of God which emerges when God is interpreted in a metaphysics of *process* as over against a metaphysics of static being; the other involves the principle that all knowledge, without exception, is derived from a critical interpretation of what is given in human experience.

"That which thou canst comprehend is not God," says St. Augustine, and one can only say, Amen.[2] No system of metaphysics can exhaust the meaning of God for us or answer all our questions about the mode of His being. But the Creator God of Christian theology is involved in basic structures which underlie everything that is, so that we ought to be able to find traces of His presence in this moving scheme of things. God is present to us as that reality which makes it possible for the world to exist, and for it to be a world in which living, conscious, responsible beings can find meaning, freedom, and worth in life.

Under the impact of modern science our world view has been shifting in the past three hundred years. A new metaphysical orientation has emerged. It finds varied expression in the philosophies of Whitehead, Bergson, Wieman, Hartshorne and others, in which the concept of process is held to be the most general and fundamental idea which we can apply to anything we know. To be anything is to be an active functioning reality entering into dynamic relations with other things. Now a philosophical theology which takes process as its basic category has one supreme advantage over the metaphysical systems in which Christian thought has traditionally been expressed. This philosophy makes it possible for the Living God, the God who acts, the caring, saving God of the Bible to be made intelligible. The liberal theology has never yet been given sufficient credit for having taken the new science—the new world view of the nineteenth century, the conception of growth, and evolving life—and trying to reconceive the nature of God so as to make His relation to such a world intelligible. To think of God as acting in dynamic relation to His creatures not merely as one actor among many, but as the universal creative power which sustains all things, and without which they could neither be nor act, is true to what our best knowledge of the world tells us. It is true to the insight of the Bible, which the philosophical tradition has tended to obscure behind the impassive mask of absolute, static being.

On this point there is considerable agreement in contemporary Protestant theology, even among those who claim to reject all philosophic approach to the knowledge of God. To put the same point in theological terms, the immutability and the impassivity of God are notions which hide from us the creative loving God. The doctrine that only the human nature of Jesus and not the divine nature suffered on the cross is a Catholic dogma against which the inward spirit of Protestant thought rebels. Emil Brunner is one of those who hold that the Christian doctrine of creation is not to be interpreted as a general philosophic concept; but he surely is stating the same point we have made when he says:

The created world is not simply the world, but the world-from-God, the world in which God is present and operating. . . . There is no divine creation which is not as such also a divine manifestation and a divine presence at work.[3]

When we say that something of the nature of God is disclosed to us in the basic order of things which embraces our human life, the problem of the transcendence and immanence of God in relation to the world is immediately involved. The conception of God as immanent in the world order was one of the ideas by which nineteenth-century theology sought to get God back into the world from which a strictly Darwinian interpretation of the natural processes would seem to have excluded Him. But what it can mean to say that God is *immanent* in the world without an intolerable spatializing of the concept was never made clear.

It is difficult to think of either immanence or transcendence without falling into such crude and irrelevant conceptions as "being spatially contained in," "being outside of." Professor Karl Heim's *God Transcendent* might be thought to offer some help as he brilliantly shows how the concept of transcendence and its related concept, that of a boundary, can be applied to relations between persons. The boundary between I and Thou is something more than a line between the spaces we occupy. But in the last pages of his work Heim declares that God's transcendence of the world is entirely different from all meanings of transcendence drawn from human experience. How has it helped Heim as theologian then to have gone through the whole philosophical discussion of transcendence since theology can make nothing of it? This question about Heim's position has been incisively raised by Miss Dorothy M. Emmet in her excellent *The Nature of Metaphysical Thinking*.[4]

In contrast to Heim I am asserting that concepts drawn from our human experience do illuminate God's way of being in relation to us. Evidence is found in the analysis of transcendence and immanence which Professor Charles Hartshorne has made. He shows how the metaphysics of process can resolve some of the ancient problems. He says:

I deny that any traditional definition of transcendence—or, for that matter, of immanence—is unambiguous. According to current metaphysics every individual is immanent in and transcends all others, and the transcendence and immanence of God is the supreme case of this double relation.[5]

To exist as a real thing is surely to possess some measure of independence, some "self-hood" which prevents absolute domination by other things. This is true of every atom of existence. This particular atom is unique, and not even God makes it something that it is not. But every individual in so far as things enter into mutually determinative relations, enters into the determination of the constitution of everything else.[6]

To transcend something is to be independent of it, to be immanent in something is to have one's own being enter directly into the constitution of that thing. As Professor Hartshorne has brilliantly shown, the consequences of this analysis for our thought of God's relationship to the world are far-reaching. The God who is the supreme determinant of the nature of all things, entering into their very constitution sustains the relation of immanence to every creature. But it is equally true to say that God transcends every creature, in a way which is incomparably greater than their "independence of him." For God does not depend upon any particular creatures for His own being. He is the ground of the metaphysical order which makes all particular creatures possible.[7]

This formulation of the doctrine of transcendence and immanence, shows, I think, why the statement that "God is in us" is not appropriate in theology. It would seem to identify God with some human tendency, or aspect of our being, for example—with the will to the good in man, as Professor Garnett has it.[8] This is not only an erroneous notion, but is dangerous to religion, as will be shown in the argument that follows. God is indeed in us, in the sense that His goodness and power enter into the determination of our life and action. Our goodness is a response to His, and exists only in dependence upon it. But God's goodness is never to be identified with our will and our ideals as they are. Immanence means "entering into the determination of," not "identification with." What may seem like an abstract problem in metaphysics here becomes a most practical issue in the Christian life. The subtle temptation to worship ourselves, to identify our ideals and plans with God's good is just what the contemporary Barthian protest so rightly challenges in the liberal theology. But a more careful analysis of the conception of God's immanence shows that we can make a radical distinction between God and ourselves without falling into the error of making a complete separation between Him and His creatures.

All metaphysical formulations are difficult, and lead to further discussion. But the fundamental pattern of our thought about God is, I trust, becoming clear. The God who saves us is neither the wholly transcendent absolute, the unmoved mover, nor is He merely the inward working power among other powers of the simple theology of immanence. He is what He is, in His own integrity, the everlasting source of all being and good, present in every moment of the world's life, determining it as fully as it can be determined in the light of the fact that out of His love He has set His creatures free, and will not destroy their freedom.

This conception of God leads us directly to the second of our basic presuppositions, that which concerns our knowledge of God. The God who is present to us can be known through our direct experience of Him. This is a radical assertion. It establishes the resemblance of our standpoint to some types of Christian thought, and cuts us off sharply from others. We certainly cannot make any such claim without analyzing it carefully and without recognizing the real difficulties involved.

In simplest statement, the position of the experiential theology is that we know God in the same fundamental manner that we know anything else: by interpreting our immediate experience to discover

what realities are impinging upon us. We know a chair, for example, by having a direct experience of the chair as it enters into
our field of vision and of touch. We do not experience merely the
idea of the chair as the idealists have it, nor the essence of some
third entity between us and the chair as the critical realists have
it. We experience this particular chair as it exists in the swirling
field of force which impinges upon us and causes us to see, feel,
perhaps alter our path. This is realism, naïve if you like, but it is
the most plausible and down-to-earth assumption we can make.
Further, no refinement of philosophical criticism has shown that
it is an erroneous assumption. Our position departs from naïve
realism in this, however, that we see the chair in perspective. Our
sense organs are selectors as well as perceptors. Or better—perception is selection. Out of the mass of stimuli which comes to us, only
those register in our awareness which can effectively enter into the
constitution of such an organism as ours. There is much of the
chair that escapes our senses, our knowledge. We know that. And
we know that we can make mistakes, perhaps, think we see a chair
when none is there. But this statement makes no sense, unless there
is some way of finding out within the limits of human fallibility
that there are times when we do not make a mistake.

Now this realistic theory gives us an analogy for our knowledge
of God. We know God when through a critical reflection upon our
experience we discover impinging upon us that pervasive creative
ground of our being which binds us to one another and to all things
as sharers in real good. I am agreeing with John Baillie in his
sensitive treatment of this problem of knowledge of God:

> I believe the view to be capable of defence that no one of the four sub-
> jects of our knowledge—ourselves, our fellows, the corporeal world, and
> God—is ever presented to us except in conjunction with all three of the
> others.[9]

If this be true, the problem of knowing God is that of discernment. We must so clarify our interpretation of what is presented

to us in experience that we can begin to trace, however inadequately, the outlines of that which stands "beyond, behind, and within, the passing flux of immediate things."[10]

While we contend that our knowledge of God is derived from experience just as is our knowledge of all other realities, there are two highly important respects in which our knowledge of God differs from all other knowledge. These differences need to be sharply set forth. In the first place, God is infinitely greater, more complex, more hidden, more beyond the grasp of our minds than any or all of His creatures. We do but touch the hem of His garment. If in our experience of the meanest flower that blows we are overawed with the mystery and the inexhaustible glory of this intricate bit of creation, how much more must we confess our inadequate understanding of God. It is true there is one point of human history where the obscure God becomes more luminous than anywhere else, in the face of Jesus Christ, and we shall speak of the significance of that knowledge in a moment. But here, too, we must say that the meaning of Jesus Christ is not for us simply and completely comprehensible. He is indeed the inexhaustible revelation of God. The tradition in Protestant theology of the "hiddenness" of God in Christ is truer to our Christian experience than is the objectively recognizable sign-performing God-Man of Roman Catholic theology.

The second special characteristic of our knowledge of God is that in Him we are seeking to know that reality which pervades all particular realities, and not something which is like the chair, limited to one locus in space and time. In one sense this would seem to make God easier to know than anything else. "Nearer is he than breathing, and closer than hands or feet." But even our commonest human experience tells us that the things which most pervade our experience—the love of those about us, the deepest hopes which lure us, the all-embracing order of nature—these just because they are ever present can remain mysteriously hidden, even forgotten.

So also with God's presence. Perhaps the best analogy is that with our experience of time and space. Surely if anything is omnipresent to our experience it is these two orders, yet to see them clearly for what they are has been very nearly the despair of all human philosophy. The whole history of philosophy can be written from the standpoint of the effort of man to clarify and integrate his conceptions of time and space as they enter into the constitution of the world. It is not an accident that in this story of philosophy, the problem of God has been closely related to the problem of space and time. In both cases we are seeking to grasp something which underlies the structure of the world. St. Augustine's superb chapter (XI) in his *Confessions* is the classic example. As with the guidance of this supreme Christian philosopher we try to find our way into the mystery of time and its companion, memory, we feel at last that we are lying in the lap of God and looking up into the face of His eternity. We see a little. We know that God is there. We know what it means to be a creature, sharing in a creation which flows from a source which never ceases its active working. Yet we are perfectly ready to say with St. Augustine, "That which thou comprehendest, is not God," if comprehension means any complete and adequate grasp.

Our claim that we know God directly in experience can be made without presuming that this knowledge is easily had, or ever more than dimly possessed. We cannot prove God's existence as we would that of the chair, saying lo here, lo there. How easy it is for man to overlook God! On this point I believe that John Baillie takes a mistaken position in the book already quoted. I have agreed with him that God is present to all experience; but it is not necessary to agree with him that "all men believe in God" if not with the top of their minds, certainly with the bottom of their hearts. It may be so, but it is surely an impossible thing to prove. What seems more likely is that disbelief in God is possible for man. God does not shout His presence at us.

One consequence of basic importance for Christian thought can be drawn from this analysis. Since God is the hidden, incomprehensible, infinitely difficult end of our human quest, whether or not we come to know Him depends ultimately upon whether God Himself so acts upon us that He produces the kind of sensitivity through which we can respond to Him.

The important implication for our interpretation of the Christian experience of God can now be summarily stated. We know God as present to us in all experience. But all our human knowing comes through particular experiences. We always experience in particular ways, here and now. In short our knowledge of anything is historical. It is derived from concrete happenings through which the real order of things is disclosed to us. Every happening can yield knowledge; but knowledge depends in part on the subjective element in our encounter with the world. Where there is no sensitivity there is no experience. We ourselves have to be equipped and transformed so that we can respond to what is given to us in our total experience. Our knowledge of God is the case par excellence of this necessity for sensitive discrimination and responsiveness. There are conditions of mind and spirit for recognizing the presence of God, as there are analogous conditions for recognizing the structure, the beauty, and the spirit of a symphony. But the question of what conditions we can specify for sensitivity to God's reality is an exceedingly delicate one. One may rightly ask whether we can specify any conditions whatever. Some indeed appeal to us in these days who say it is only the despair of all human knowing and experience, which may open our minds to God.

There is a way of stating the case here. The search of the mystics for a discipline, a regimen by which the soul may mount to the vision of God, is a valid search. The pure in heart shall see God, and purity of heart is something which we can seek, and provide conditions for realizing. But where the mystical effort fails is in supposing that this human preparation in itself can bring us to see

God, or even that as human effort it can bring us closer to God. That is a very great error. The danger is we forget our radical dependence upon God in all our knowing. All knowledge of God that is recognition—and not merely cognition—of His reality, is a gift which is given by the working of God Himself in our life.

One further statement about the discovery of God is necessary. That which gives us as Christians the possibility of recognizing God is the fact that we share in a living stream of historical experience in which God has disclosed Himself. This stream of experience begins with the Hebrew people. Its supreme events were the experiences of that people as interpreted by the prophets. The prophets were not infallible on matters of fact, or in political judgment, or even in religious insight. But they traced through the tragic life of their people the divine working of judgment, of healing, and of mercy, and they recognized the Lordship of the righteous God over all life. In Jesus of Nazareth the expectation of the Messiah received an unexpected and revolutionary fulfillment. A new people was born who had seen God in a human life, and who henceforth could understand the meaning of life only by seeing it in the light which came from the impact of Jesus upon men. To speak of revelation in the prophets and in Christ is not to speak then of some supernatural doctrine added to our human knowledge from an extrahistorical source. It is to speak of those happenings in human history which have so opened our eyes, and so transformed our minds that the disclosure of God to man has taken place.

What we shall try to say now about God and His gracious working for our good cannot be proved as a theorem. It is an interpretation of life based upon the experience of the Christian community. To share in the life of this community, to do its work, to hear its story, to read its Book, is the way to such knowledge of God as Christians have. We are not claiming exclusive knowledge of God for Christians. Nowhere has He left Himself without witness.[11] We are not claiming that what we have seen and testify to in our Christian experience is all the truth. What we do argue is that the human search for knowledge of the ultimate metaphysical truths, that is, for the reality on which all things depend for their being, and the Christian attempt to clarify what we have found disclosed to us in Christ, are two complementary sides of the same story, the story of God's self-disclosure to the mind of man. There is one God, and the truth about Him must finally be the same for the philosopher who is a lover of wisdom as it is for the Christian believer who finds the Divine Logos in Christ.[12]

II

Say then that our theological task is to set forth how it is that God's dealing with man can be described from the standpoint of Christian experience. When we say there is a creative and a redemptive work of God going on in human history what is the content of our words? What specifically are the activities of creation and redemption, and what are the demands they lay upon us?

God's creation is His making the world, and His leading it toward fuller, finer life. Of the warp of space and the woof of time this existence of ours is woven, and held together in a dynamic whole. This does not commit us to the doctrine that this world-whole is an *organic* unity as we know it. It seems not to be, but rather appears as a fluid order with all sorts of variety, looseness, types of structure, ragged edges, clashing swirling power.[13] But to be anything at all is to share in the total society of being. Whatever the truth in pluralism, there is this truth in monism: no world without a fundamental order which makes it a world.

This creation contains a thrust toward more complex, richer orders. To be a living thing is to become, to reach out restlessly, unceasingly, and in some measure creatively toward new life and new order. God is that reality in and through all things which makes possible the response of life to the lure of fulfillment beyond the present.[14]

God the Creator we know as the power which binds the surging variety of life into richer and wider societies of mutual enjoyment and support. To be anything is to enter into social relations. Perhaps this is even true of electrons; it certainly is true of all living things, and supremely of men. But the good life is woven into these social relations. A purely individual and absolutely isolated enjoyment of appreciation is nothing at all. Emil Brunner defined hell in a recent lecture as being "the state of absolute loneliness." It is in the shared enjoyments and appreciations of social experience that real value emerges. God makes life good by creating communities in which life is so related to life that all the enjoyments, powers, and appreciations of each individual enhance the good of all the other members of the community. This is to see God's presence in that

> dark
> Inscrutable workmanship that reconciles
> Discordant elements, makes them cling together
> In one society.[15]

While we affirm the creative work of God, in world-making, world-binding, and world-leading toward new communities of good, we have not identified God's activity with the whole process of life. The poet's "Some call it evolution, and others call it God" was a sincere expression of religious feeling; but it ignored the fact of evil. What we have said is that through the vast mystery of the whole world-process we are able to see the pervasive presence of the divine activity which makes this world the habitation of God's creatures and, in some measure, of His good. More than this we cannot say about the total process of nature.

We are not the creator, but we can participate in and serve the work of creation. What we create will never be identical with what God is creating; but human intelligence and artistic skill and patient workmanship can serve and release His creativity. A discounting of the importance of disciplined human effort in meeting the problems of life will enfeeble any faith or religion, and it is not Christian. Reverence for the courageous intelligent response of human beings to the problems and demands of life, the patient discipline of the scientist, the integrity and creative expression of the artist, is a valid theme of Christian theology. If we discount it we fail to recognize what God has done in creating free beings whose resources He must enlist in the fight against evil.

III

What can faith say, then, in the face of real evil? This, that there is a divine strategy of redemption. There are four primary ways in which the redemptive activity of God becomes real to us. The first is in the destruction which He visits upon intolerable evil. It may appear strange to subsume the wrath of God, for that is what this means, under redemption; but the truth which we have to learn all over again is that without wrath there is no redemption. Wrath is not vengeance, not in the human resentful sense of that term. Wrath means that *life has within it certain ineluctable structural principles which can be defied only at the risk of losing the good of life itself.* When these are defied there is set in motion, whether in an individual life or in the social order, a chain of consequences which may take the form of vast destruction and misery; or which may work silently in the individual soul in the loss of the meaning of life, the fading of the glory,—but it happens. Here is Lillian Smith's description of what we have done to ourselves in America by trying to fence off one race from another:

We white people got into deep trouble long ago when we attempted to enslave other human beings. A trouble we have never faced fully and never tried with all our strength to solve. Instead, we have tried to push it away from us, and in trying, we have used a mechanism so destructive that it . . . has become a menace to the health of our culture and our individual souls. Segregation is a way of life that is actually a form of cultural schizophrenia. . . . It is a little chilling to note the paranoid symptoms of those among us who defend segregation; their violence, their sensitiveness to criticism, their over-esteem of themselves, their desire to withdraw from everything hard to face.[16]

The wrath of God works silently and swiftly, and because we are as insensitive as we are it is usually only when we have brought catastrophe on ourselves that we recognize it at all.

The second affirmation is that God's redemption means the transmutation of evil and loss into new good, and higher fulfillment. There is a traditional doctrine that all evil, all pain, all suffering finally is used by God for His greater glory and our highest good. I doubt that we can say this on the basis of what we know.[17] There does seem to be a real loss in life, else it is hard to see what the moral struggle and the costly sacrifices of love could mean. But this we do know, that there are ways in which real evil, a shattering illness, a tragic death, or a vicious social injustice can so enter into the deeper sensitivity of men that a higher and stronger moral and spiritual power is released.

> Defeat may serve as well as victory
> To shake the soul and let the glory out.[18]

We know this is strangely true even of moral defeat. The lesson of our dependence upon God; the fatuousness of our thinking of ourselves more highly than we ought to think comes hard. But there is an illumination and we can know that there is a patient, redemptive reality in and through all of life which transmutes real evil, real loss, real threats to the growth of human good into the deeper, more sensitive and more enduring goods of love and humility.[19]

Something more is necessary if we are to live with any real hope. Man, the free creature of God, who misuses his freedom, must know God's forgiveness. That every man needs forgiveness, and that forgiveness is offered to every man, is the truth of the Gospel which is the hardest for us to accept. To believe this requires the acknowl-

edgment in humility of God's judgment. Yet it is absolutely necessary, for none of us is beyond this need.

The forgiveness of God is not a favor granted occasionally when
we happen to need it; it is a continuing quality of His love which
can hold our life together even in moral defeat. An analogy from
human experience will help to clarify this. Forgiveness in human
relations is something more than a series of particular acts of forgiveness. Jane Addams, who saw very deeply into human nature,
expressed it when she said that in all wholesome human relations
there is a forgiveness in advance. Human love, when it discovers its
essence, discovers the spirit of reconciliation. There is the human
counterpart of the mercy in the love of God, belief in which constitutes the heart of evangelical Christian faith. We come to know
the forgiveness of God primarily through those personal relationships in which love is experienced as a mercy in which we are
moved by a power greater than ourselves. The Ritschlian theology
won a truth for Protestant theology which ought never to be obscured when it made clear that the Christian community exists as
that company of people who have experienced the forgiveness of
God through what has come to them in Jesus.[20] Jesus is the person
through whom the mercy of God has been mediated to us men in
our history. That is the fact. Josiah Royce with a quite different
philosophical orientation from Ritschl expressed the same truth
when he described the Church as the community which is sustained
by its memory of the atoning deed of Jesus.[21] What is supremely
important here is that our knowledge of God's forgiveness does not
depend upon a private and subjective illumination of the individual
believer alone. It arises in the shared experience of the community
of those who through Jesus of Nazareth and what has followed upon
his life have discovered that God stands by man even when man is
in the wrong. To stand by the wrongdoer and to suffer redemptively
the consequences of his wrong is the meaning of forgiveness.

The liberal interpretation of the Gospel rarely did justice to the place of the divine forgiveness in human life. The liberal thesis that "the meaning of God in human experience" is the struggle of our better selves for moral mastery,[22] should be qualified. God saves us from moral defeat by making it possible for us to know that the love which claims us is a love which forgives and remakes us in spite of our defeats in the moral struggle.

There is a final aspect of the work of redemption. It concerns the fate of the precious values of life and personality in the "perpetual perishing" of time and death. Whether we can believe that nothing valuable is ever wholly lost in the moving stream of time, we need not say. Quite possibly our human experience does not yield an answer. But Christian faith and human experience reveal that there is a treasuring of the passing goods of life, as each passing event gives itself to and becomes a part of the ongoing movement of life, and as every movement of time finds its particular niche in eternity. The limits of this redemption of good from the wreck of time through the possible participation of each moment in the eternal totality of all moments escapes our sight. But we do know that the past is embodied in the future. We do know, though to be sure this statement needs interpretation and defense in an analysis of the nature of time, that God's "abidingness" in eternity is the necessary counterpart of His activity in time. The fact that something must persist through all time if time itself is to have any meaning is accepted by many thinkers who do not necessarily accept the presuppositions of Christian theology. Lewis Mumford, for example, affirms man's participation in eternity:

Man's earthly life, in short, involves the existence of another transcendental world: a world of durable meanings and values that in time detach themselves from the flux of history and loose their narrow ties to time and place.[23]

Mumford's term "detachment" would in the view here adopted have to be qualified. God never allows the world to become completely detached from Himself; nor would a realm of a value completely severed from time and space have meaning for us. But there is detachment from the circumstances of particular times and places in the sense that particular values exemplify qualities and patterns which are of universal significance. The values of the symphonies of Mozart and the moral insight of Lincoln had to become embodied in actual material structures, that is, in the score of the symphony and in the acts of the man Lincoln, before they were real values. Once this beauty and this moral courage have become flesh and blood in our spatiotemporal world, the whole realm of value is thereby enhanced forever, for what is particular in these individual cases represents the concretion for all time of what before was only "possibility." We do not go beyond the bounds of what Christian experience has asserted if we say that God's own being is qualified by whatever of good or ill has taken place among His creatures. God's love does not change. But the "career" of His love in His dealing with the world involves a continual sifting of the evil from the good, a creative thrust toward a more complete exemplification of His good in existence, and, it is possible to believe, a treasuring for all time of the good which does come to be.

We keep our vision of God most nearly steady if we do not say that either His creative or His redemptive working is prior to the other in the disclosure He makes of Himself to us. Certainly the fullest knowledge of the Creator comes only through the encounter with the Redeemer. But truth about God's goodness and power is revealed everywhere in the natural setting of human life, and this knowledge is not wholly perverted by sin. We stand by the validity of Paul's declaration in Romans 1:19-20 that God's majesty and power are visible in the creation, and in Romans 2:14-15 that the law of God has been written on the heart of those who have no knowledge of His revelation to the prophets of Israel.

IV

Our description so far of these aspects of God's work in the world is all prologue to the claim now to be stated which goes beyond what either liberalism or neo-orthodoxy have clearly affirmed. God does transform rebellious and self-sufficient men into persons who can begin to love their fellows. The power which works this transformation is released in the depth of personal life just at the point at which man finds his own self-righteousness shattered, and discovers that the mercy of God comes to him in his need. "If any man be in Christ he is a new creature,"[24] says Paul. Here is the Gospel announced as it must be in the indicative mood and present tense. The consummation of the new life is to be sure always in some way beyond the actual. We are "saved by hope."[25] But the ground of hope is the reality of release from that despair which robs even suffering of its meaning, the discovery of a new gratitude for life, the fact of a new humility, and the power of the will to begin to respond to the demands of life in the spirit of love. The personal discovery of the transforming mercy of God is the supreme source of power for the life of moral responsibility and creativity.

To state a belief does not prove it. The question of what evidence supports this Christian faith is full of subtle difficulties. No one description of the Christian life can do justice to all its complexities, to its continuing involvement in sin while it has yet begun to become whole. But here I am simply trying to say what it is that the Gospel is about. If the doctrine of the new life of the Christian is the hardest of all to believe, as in our disillusioned time it must be, still there can be no good news of Christ apart from the possibility that in some measure the life of love can actually be lived on this dark and bloody battlefield of human history.

Whatever the difficulties in making belief in the new life convincing, we can try to remove some misunderstandings of it. It should be underscored that the new life which flows from the experience of the redeeming mercy of God is a life of free creative effort in which all human powers are released from the shackles of a false piety and a crabbed moralism. A comment upon Dr. Eugene W. Lyman's wise and balanced philosophy of religion may sharpen the point I am urging on the relation of redemption and creativity in life. Dr. Lyman says:

> When one is seeking a point of view for a unified interpretation of religion the creative functioning of religion offers more promise than its redemptive functioning. For when creative religion confronts definite evils it inevitably becomes redemptive, whereas the transition from the redemptive functioning to the creative is not so inevitable.[26]

Now surely neither transition is *inevitable*. Religion which stresses man's creative power may become self-righteous and futile in the presence of tragic situations. Too much of the social gospel message failed precisely here. Certainly the experience of redemption may be drawn into the quicksand of moral and spiritual complacency. But the uniquely creative element in Christian experience is just the overflow of new life and power which come from the depths of that experience in which our human despair is met by the suffering love of God in all its majesty, humility, and holiness. Some of the evidence here lies in what the themes of the Incarnation, the Cross, and the Resurrection of the Christ who took upon himself the form of a servant have done to release cultural energies in Western civilization. We need only to recall the way in which the Christian drama of redemption has given life and passion to the creative arts, to painting, to music, to social ritual, and to the most difficult of all arts, those of doing good and securing justice.[27] The secret of Christianity's contribution to the cultural works of man is that in the Christian faith, with a clarity found in no other, we see that all of life, its evil as well as its good, has a meaning which supports an ultimate hope, if we but accept the truth which God has offered in Christ and begin to respond to it.

V

There is a word in the Christian vocabulary which expresses and covers the whole activity of God in human existence—the word "grace." "By the grace of God," we say, thus paying sometimes a half-conscious tribute in secular speech to our ultimate dependence upon Him. The word "grace" has been almost ruined for many thoughtful Christians because it has been mistakenly interpreted as if it means the sheer mercy of God descending upon man apart from any moral demand or human effort. But a doctrine of grace which destroys the freedom and moral responsibility of man is not the grace known in mature Christian experience. The New Testament emphasis is upon grace as forgiveness, but never as a substitute for repentance in its ethical dimensions. Now while grace means forgiveness, it is also the Christian term for the whole of God's love in action. As Dr. Moffatt says: "*Charis* had been long upon the lips of men, and always . . . it had been one of the shining words that serve the world. Beauty, kindness, gratitude; charm, favour, thankfulness. These were the main facets of the fresh word."[28] Another theologian summarizes the Christian use of the term: "Grace is the supreme causal agency by which Christian life everywhere is evoked, sustained, and augmented."[29] The Edinburgh ecumenical conference provided this statement which could form the basis for the meeting of all Christian minds:

The meaning of divine grace is truly known only to those who know that God is love, and that all that he does is done in love in fulfillment of his righteous purposes. His grace is manifested in our creation, preservation, and all the blessings of this life, but above all in our redemption through the life, death, and resurrection of Jesus Christ.[30]

All Christian doctrine of the revelation of God in Jesus Christ is an attempt to say how the unity and the power of God's saving activity are experienced in the impact of that one life upon mankind. Christ is the climax of creation, the incarnation of the Logos without which nothing is made, the restoration of the image of God, the divine love made real in a human spirit. But this is also a world in which Christ is crucified. Redemption must come on the other side of the rent in the creation, exposed by man's rejection of love. God invades human history at the cost of suffering. Redemption is won as men find themselves judged, forgiven, and brought to repentance through the fact of God's victory on the cross.

The grace of God is no simple solution to the plight of man. The Christian faith does not offer solutions in the utilitarian sense of that term. It offers new life, and power, and faith. The rediscovery of the meaning of grace has come to our time through the way of agony and despair. It remains for evangelical Christianity to state again with power the faith that grace is present, available, victorious over evil. We must show how we rightly understand our human history when we see the sign of the cross in all of it and over all of it. Then the Gospel will do for our time what it has done before to

> rally the lost and trembling forces of the will,
> gather them up, and let them loose upon the earth.[31]

CHAPTER THREE

Man's Real Good

WHAT makes the Christian Gospel good news is its proclamation of the reality of God's redeeming grace. A new life can come into being within the present wrong and failure, the bitter injustice and despair. There is a divine strategy for achievement of new good in the midst of stubborn evil. Such is the conviction which we have set forth in the last chapter.

It is one thing to state a conviction, and quite another to show that it will stand when brought up against the facts of human experience. It is, literally, an infinite task to show that a theological perspective can solve the knotty problems of nature and law, ethics and politics, life and death, and bring them all within an interpretation which possesses an intelligible unity. Yet however difficult this task, and however far from realization it must be in our time and perhaps in every time, to try to fulfill this demand is the obligation which Christian thought must accept for itself. Christian truth is not a separate truth within the whole meaning of life. Christian teaching cannot be put into an intellectual hot house and there kept safe from the chilling blasts which blow in our human journey. If belief in the creative and the redemptive God makes sense at all, it must enable us to see more deeply and clearly into the whole of our experience, and to find what in the end of the day all honest thought must find there.

In this and the following two chapters we must deal with three of the fundamental problems which are involved in any assertion of the Christian faith in redemption. The first of these is the question of how we can adequately define that love which Christianity holds to be the clue to the nature of God and therefore define the content of that real good in relation to which all particular goods are finally judged. The second question concerns the relation of love as the ultimate ideal to the actual structures of nature and human social institutions. In particular we shall examine the problem of the Christian ideal of love when it is confronted by the realities of the political orders. Thirdly, we must show the implications of the doctrine that love is the real good for the Christian interpretation of the progress of the Kingdom of God in history. We shall state, at the close of Chapter Five, the clue to the Christian view of history to which our analysis leads. We shall then be ready to consider the positive implications of this theological perspective in which the creative and the redemptive work of God are affirmed together, for Christian ethics, for Christian politics, and for the life of the spirit when the Christian commitment becomes a way of meeting both life and death.

At the start of our analysis of the Christian "idea of the good," we may notice that this problem is directly related to one which will already have occurred to the reader. How is God one? How do we know that the various processes of creativity and redemption are all manifestations of one single reality? If we cannot show the unity of God, then we have no saving truth; for the problem of life is to find that unity and wholeness in the nature of things to which we can give ourselves with single-minded devotion. I believe it can be shown that the only convincing answer to the problem of unity in our world view lies in the discovery of one intelligible structure which is the pattern of the real good of all things. This real good is not our creation. It is that growing good which we find partly realized, partly stretching beyond existence as an unrealized ideal. We discover its claim upon us whenever we think the problem of the value of life through to the end. The thesis I defend in this chapter can be put in three brief sentences: God's unity is His goodness. God's goodness is His love. God's love is that creative and redemptive power which works unceasingly in all times and places to bring to fulfillment a universal community of free and loving beings.

Let us begin with an exploratory definition of the "good."

I

To define the good is one of the perennial problems of human life. Plain men and philosophers have sought for a valid concept of the good, have been perplexed by the search, and have arrived at many different conclusions. It would be simple if we could say from the Christian standpoint that there is a fixed definition of the good, but we have to recognize that here Christianity has always revealed an inner tension. That tension arises from the fact that Christianity has always conceived this created world as essentially good, and yet it has always looked beyond this world to a consummation of life in a new order as man's true end. Professor Amos Wilder justly observes that this tension has never been resolved. "The Christian has not made clear for himself the paradox of world denial and abundance of life. He has lodged in an otherworldliness that has seemed, whether to a Nietzsche or a Lawrence, a blasphemy against the natural creation, or in a compromise with life that has lost any creative appeal, and so deserved the apostasy of those thirsty for reality."[1]

If we look at the principal symbols with which Christianity has expressed the meaning of human fulfillment, we see how this perplexity about man's true good pervades Christian experience. The primary symbol is the Kingdom of God. But in the New Testament the Kingdom appears as a reality experienced in the present, "The kingdom of heaven is among you"; and at the same time as other than this present order, "My kingdom is not of this world."[2] Again,

Christianity says it is the abundant life which Christ offers. While it is never said that the abundant life means a denial of the goods of this world, yet it really consists in the laying up of the soul's treasure in heaven; hence, the central paradox, "Whosoever would save his life shall lose it, and whosoever shall lose his life for my sake and the gospel's shall save it."[3] The term "eternal life" seems to point rather more unambiguously to the fulfillment of the good in life beyond death, yet in the fourth gospel, for which this is the central symbol, eternal life means a relationship to God in which man participates in this world. Here and now he may pass from death unto life.[4]

The New Testament term "love," *agape*, is that on which the whole Christian faith finally rests, for "God is love."[5] Love is the content of the Kingdom, and it is the power of God's love which brings the world into the Kingdom. Eternal life means life in the eternal love of God. Now this love by which and for which man is created, this love which constitutes the final good for which the creative and redemptive power of God is poured out, is revealed in Christ. For the answer to the question, "What is good?" the Christian looks at God's revelation in Jesus Christ. Christ is the restoration of the true image of man, because he is the incarnation of the love which is the meaning of our existence.

The problem of defining the ultimate good in Christian theology thus becomes that of interpreting as explicitly as possible the meaning of the *agape* disclosed in Christ. Thus the issues which are being debated anew in the theological turmoil today center in the meaning of Christian love as it points on the one side to the possibilities of human existence, and as it points on the other side to a fulfillment of this life in an ultimate good which transcends the possibilities of this world.

The problem we are attacking can be formulated in the following way: Can it be shown that the interests of man, the creature, and the earthly efforts of man to increase values in this life, bear a positive relation to the work of God's love looking toward His Kingdom? It might seem that the answer is simple. We have said that God's love is not a denial of this world. If He seeks the good for His creatures, surely every human achievement is a contribution to God's goal. But the matter is not so simple. Beginning with the experience of Paul, the Christian view of this world which came to theological expression in the Reformers and which has now been revived with great power in the contemporary Protestant theology, has always shown a certain distrust of identifying human efforts toward the good with the divine work of redemption on the ground that the good as man knows it and seeks it is really of a different order from the good revealed in Christ. No human love, it is held, even the most idealistic, can be said to embody *agape*, the love of God, for human love is always limited and ambiguous in its object, and is corrupted by human selfishness in its essential spirit. "Man's altruism and idealism are not only unreliable but also in the nature of the human case bound to the chariot of self-interest."[6] If this be the truth of man's situation, then we must make a sharp distinction between God's work of redemption and all the manifold workings of human culture. The achievement of the artist, the philosopher, the artisan, the politician are not disparaged in themselves, but we must not confuse them with the divine working which is of another order. But if our thesis that the work of redemption *includes* a work of creation in which human creative effort shares is valid, then this radical separation between the divine love and man's works of love must be shown to be a distortion of the fact. I wish to show that when Christian faith points to the Kingdom of God's love as the ultimate good, it is pointing to a reality which cannot be absolutely separated from the imperfect goods for which men strive.

It is the possibility of holding to this unitary structure of the good wherever we find it in all the realms of human interest and value that makes it possible to integrate our conception of God with an ultimate standard of judgment for all particular values. To achieve this interpretation is, I suggest, the only true and saving answer to the quest of the Christian mind for unity in thought and life. The order of value which is defined by love is the unifying fact, partly realized, partly stretching beyond realization as a possibility, to which we can give our allegiance completely. It is the nature of God Himself.

The neo-orthodox school in theology today stands against this position. It insists that the love of God is of a radically different order from all human love and human values, and however these two orders are to be related they cannot be brought into a single structure. If we are to maintain our position it must be against this contrary view. Let us examine then two of the most powerful statements of it, those of Bishop Anders Nygren and of Reinhold Niebuhr, for I believe them to be in error and that error underlies much of the distortion in the Christian interpretation of man's predicament into which we are being led. If the views of these theologians are correct, then the good accomplished in redemption lies in a different dimension from the good realized by human effort, and we cannot sustain the thesis that the work of redemption involves as an integral aspect a process in this world, and the actualization of love in this life.

II

Bishop Nygren, in his great work, *Agape and Eros,* aims to set forth what he calls the fundamental motif of Christianity which distinguishes it from the *nomos* motif of Judaism and the *eros* motif of Hellenism.[7] The *motif,* in the view of Professor Nygren's school of historical study, means the answer which a religion gives to the most fundamental questions which can be asked concerning the way of salvation. In Judaism man becomes acceptable to God through conformity to God's law, for God loves the righteous man. In

Hellenistic religion, taking its inspiration from Plato, it is love as *eros* which leads man to God. *Eros* here is not carnal love, but rather the ascent of the soul out of the realm of the flesh toward God, who is true and absolute being. God draws man as the object of desire draws the one who desires. Man finds salvation and immortality by rising on the wings of *eros* into the being of God. The Christian motif is that of salvation through love, but this is the love which is named *agape* in the New Testament. It must be distinguished absolutely, according to Professor Nygren, from *eros*. *Agape* is the love of God coming down to sinful man. It is spontaneous, unmotivated, poured out for man without regard to merit. Man has no worth which gives him a claim upon the love of God, either before it is given or afterward.[8] Man is brought into fellowship with God, but this is not the fellowship as in the *eros* way of holy men with a God to whom their holiness makes them acceptable, but it is fellowship of a forgiving God with forgiven sinners. *Agape* is completely self-giving love. God has given himself in Christ and thus makes possible salvation which man cannot in any way attain for himself.

Professor Nygren believes the motif of *agape* cannot be mixed with that of *eros* any more than can fire and water. The attempt to make a synthesis of them can only result in the damaging or the utter elimination of the truth of *agape*. Actually the two have been brought together in the history of Christian thought which Professor Nygren traces so superbly in his study, but all attempts at synthesis, including that of St. Augustine with his doctrine of love as *caritas*, and that of the medieval theologians and mystics who saw the problem and tried to make a place for unselfish love within the Christian doctrine, really obscured and corrupted the fundamental Christian truth which was recovered by Luther in the Protestant Reformation.

Our question concerning Professor Nygren's work does not involve any rejection of the idea that in *agape* Christianity has a conception of God's love which does transcend other religious motifs. Today when so much of man's life lies in the shambles of physical and moral destruction, the word of a divine mercy which goes out creatively to man in love becomes the veritable rock of salvation. The question is whether the meaning of *agape* is adequately represented in Nygren's formulation. I suggest that he has overstated certain tendencies in the *agape* motif in such a way that its positive relation to human striving and ideals is obscured.

One way of dealing with a theological doctrine is to ask what the consequences are to which it leads. If these cannot be accepted, then there is at least a strong suspicion that something is wrong with it. Professor Nygren's interpretation of *agape* leads to some very curious consequences. The first is that since *agape* is given to an object not worthy of it, the Christian cannot really say that he has *agape* toward God. The whole conception of man's love to God becomes a puzzle in Nygren's view.[9] Because of certain New Testament expressions, notably the first commandment emphasized by Jesus, he must allow it, but only in a "secondary" sense, the meaning of which remains unclear. If salvation means fellowship with God, it is hard to see what this could be except mutual love in some sense between man and God.

But more than this, man cannot even want to be found by God or saved, in Professor Nygren's view, because desire for fellowship with God would be an egocentric desire and therefore man would really be cut off from God by the very fact of his desiring to find Him. It is difficult to see what Nygren would do with the beatitude, "Blessed are those which do hunger and thirst after righteousness, for they shall be filled," because according to him all hungering and thirsting is egocentric. Again in emphasizing that God's love is poured out on the just and the unjust, Nygren apparently sets aside that aspect of the New Testament message which emphasizes God's justice. He asks, "Why should God's love necessarily direct itself to that which is better?"[10] But if God's love makes no distinction as to that which is better, then it is impossible to see what the moral life is at all. Nygren's doctrine leads to a radical antinomianism. For example, with regard to the ethical ideal of altruism, he says:

> . . . the so-called love of one's neighbor, the "universal benevolence" or altruism, which, it is said, is to be retained, is in fact so far different from Christian love that it is its most fatal perversion; for even if such "humane" ideals present on the surface certain similarities with Christian love, they are built up on a wholly different foundation, and have really no connection with it at all.[11]

In cutting off *agape* from all human norms, Nygren overlooks the fact that from its beginning as disclosed in the New Testament, Christian faith has always kept a tension between God's love and justice. There is a final separation of the good from the evil, however complex and mysterious the relation between mercy and justice may be. Nygren, like Kierkegaard, apparently allows no place for growth in grace. He says explicitly there is no ascent of the Christian toward God.[12]

The final consequence of this doctrine of *agape* is that it becomes unintelligible. *Agape*, Nygren holds, is irrational.[13] Of course an irrational doctrine cannot be refuted, but then it cannot be brought into any significant relation to human experience. All of these consequences lead to the conclusion that this doctrine of *agape* is an unacceptable interpretation of the New Testament message. It sets forth the evangelical truth, but in such an extreme form as to constitute a *reductio ad absurdum* of this truth.

If we can show where Nygren's analysis has gone astray, we shall be on the way toward finding a more adequate interpretation of *agape*. His fundamental error lies in two closely related assumptions: one having to do with theological method and the other with the conception of the structure of love. As to method Nygren assumes that the basic motif of any faith must be exclusive of the motifs of other faiths. This assumption that what is significant in Christianity must be the exclusive possession of Christianity runs all through the contemporary revival of reformation theology, and it has worked much mischief. That the Christian Gospel can be unique and yet remain positively related to what is known of God in other gospels seems to be everywhere denied by contemporary theologians. But why? This self-consciousness of Christianity about its distinctive truth is understandable when the Church finds itself opposed by a demonic religion such as Nazism. But a just appreciation of God's general revelation of Himself should preserve the truth that Christianity has meaning for man precisely because it represents a fulfillment of the knowledge of God which is made possible through all the things which He has made. Nygren claims, of course, simply to be setting forth scientifically the fundamental Christian motif without arguing its truth or value against any other motif. But actually to set forth a doctrine of salvation with the assertion that this alone is Christianity and everything else a corruption of Christianity, makes a work polemical throughout. He does admit that quite possibly it was only through the conjoining of *agape* with elements of *nomos* and *eros* that *agape* could have made its way into the experience of man. But this admission in itself would certainly tend to suggest that there is a more organic bond between *agape, nomos,* and *eros* than he strictly allows.

The error Nygren makes with respect to the structure of love is related to this arbitrary exclusiveness of his method, for he assumes that love must be either purely egocentric or completely spontaneous and unmotivated, when actually all love does combine the desire of the self with the good of the other. The argument that if man desires God, his desire cannot be unselfish since it is really his own desire that he wants satisfied, is simply the old sophisticated argument against altruism. If I enjoy my neighbor's good fortune I am really selfish in this since it is I who enjoy his good fortune. The real question is, therefore, whether if I derive satisfaction from my neighbor's good, the source of my satisfaction is wholly in myself. This would be true only in one case, that is, if I and my neighbor are absolutely isolated beings. But love is possible precisely because man is a social creature. I can feel my neighbor's feelings, identify myself with his good. Nygren overlooks the fact that the relationship between man and his neighbor and between man and God is fundamentally a social relationship in which the good of one actually does become the good of the other. Nygren regards the medieval doctrine of love as friendship (*amor amicitiae*) as a curious and invalid attempt to allow for the unselfish element in love. But if man is a social creature there is nothing curious or invalid about the doctrine that I can unselfishly enjoy my neighbor's good.[14] The logic of this problem and the solution I am urging has been set forth with a clarity equal to Nygren's in Charles Hartshorne's *Man's Vision of God*.

A similar analysis must be made of Nygren's view of God's action as opposed to man's action. That the initiative remains in some way with God in all responsible human action has been maintained fairly consistently in Christian theology. But Nygren does not seem to consider that God's power can be primary and yet man can have a measure of creative freedom in himself. Interpreting Luther, Nygren says, "The Christian is not an independent center of power alongside of God. . . . He has nothing of his own to give. He is merely the tube, the channel, through which God's love flows."[15] This conclusion which utterly negates human responsibility is not necessary. It is the very mark of love to allow power to the objects of love. The tendency in modern philosophical theology to interpret God's power and man's derived power as dynamically related in the ongoing of life is fundamentally sound, however it may have been oversimplified in the liberal period.

Just how this relationship is to be expressed is a part of the problem we are attacking. But it should be pointed out that we are not bound to the errors which have been made in some of the traditional formulations. Professor Nygren gives the impression; in a few places he says quite explicitly, that all attempts to mingle *eros* with *agape*

lead directly to the self-deification, the metaphysical dualism between body and spirit, the self-righteousness of Platonism and
mysticism, and we might add, of much modern liberal theology. But
the real problem is so to formulate the relationship of God and man
as to keep clear the distinction between them and yet not fall into a
disparagement of man.

We must say, then, that there is nothing in the idea of *agape*
which excludes the element of human desire for the good. But just
here we have to admit the problem of the Christian life appears,
for is it not so that our human love is actually egocentric, that
under the guise of love to God or neighbor we insinuate our in-
ordinate self-love into our most spiritual efforts? Man's problem is
not that *agape* stands entirely outside his desire, but practically it is
that when sinful man desires he corrupts the spirit of love. That this
is an aspect of the truth about man with which Christian theology
must forever struggle, is becoming clear again in our time. To un-
mask the secret disguises of selfishness through the light of the love
of God which seeketh not its own, is the heart of the evangelical
message which Nygren's work is enabling us to recover. How can
this message be recovered in a way that does not disregard the positive worth of human effort in the sight of God? That this can be
done is my thesis.

III

It is particularly instructive to turn from Nygren's work to that of
Reinhold Niebuhr, for the latter is a theologian who sees the truth
for which Nygren is contending and yet who insists that there is a
way of bringing *agape* into a positive relation to the human struggle
for the ideals of justice and brotherhood. Niebuhr is also instructive
in this connection because it is out of his own practical acquaintance
with political and social struggles that he rediscovers the transcendent element in Christian love. Nothing can be wider of the

mark than to interpret Niebuhr as intending a complete pessimism. His aim is so to bring the Christian perspective into the concrete political and social experience of modern life that the possibility of achieving justice and brotherhood in human affairs will be increased because men are in some measure freed from the sentimental and romantic notions which can only lead to bitter disillusionment. Christian love must be seen in its positive significance for human efforts in history, and at the same time its transcendent position of judgment upon all human effort must be preserved. How is this to be done?

Niebuhr's solution consists in making a distinction between sacrificial and mutual love. Sacrificial love is *agape*. It is the self-giving love of God. It is man's final norm, his true good. Sacrificial love is forgiving. It is poured out to the other without calculating the merit of the other or reward to the self. Only such love as this, given to man by God, can redeem the inevitable failures of man's own spirit. Mutual love is good will which is reciprocated. It is the will to the good of the other, but a good in which the self participates.[16] Mutual love is not, therefore, the love which we know in God. The limit of mutual love is the inclusion of the good of the self in the good intended. Now Niebuhr holds that mutual love is possible for man. No limits to which it may be realized in wider and wider areas of brotherhood can be set.

Is sacrificial love possible for man? Here the answer seems to be: in an absolute sense it is not possible for man. The well-known phrase "impossible possibility" stands here in Niebuhr's thought for the warning that the pure love of God transcends human possibility.[17] At the same time an element of uncalculating sacrificial giving of the self to the good of the other is possible for man. Indeed Niebuhr believes that unless there is a degree of sacrificial love in human mutuality, mutuality will break down. "The self cannot achieve relations of mutual and reciprocal affection with others if its actions are dominated by the fear that they may not be reciprocated."[18] When the pure love of God appears in history in Christ, the limits of history for realizing *agape* are seen, for Christ must refuse "to participate in the claims and counterclaims of historical existence."[19] He can symbolize disinterested love only by refusing to become involved in historical rivalries. His life ends on the cross which stands at the edge of history showing man what his spirit ought to be, at the same time that it discloses what man as man cannot be. Niebuhr thus seems to have brought together the perfect love of God which transcends all selfishness with the human yearning for mutuality and the struggle of man for justice. By asserting the paradoxical relationship of sacrificial and mutual love he holds them together without identifying them. The Christian Gospel becomes a support of the human struggle for the good, a prophetic criticism of the spirit of that struggle, and a final assertion that man receives from God the forgiveness which enables him both to know and to accept his limitations.

Is this really a solution? Can Christian love be divided into two kinds of love held together only in the tenuous bonds of paradox? The great danger of this solution is that it leaves *agape* and therefore the very foundation of the Christian life fragmented and unintelligible. I do not wish to criticize the *direction* of Niebuhr's solution, for that is precisely in line with the attempt to bring the doctrine of redemption into organic relation with the realization of human good in history. But Niebuhr's *formulation* of the doctrine of love is not beyond criticism. The alternative to it can be plainly seen if we ask the simple question, "What is the good which the spirit of *agape* seeks—what does Christian love intend?" The answer to this must be in any Christian view that *agape* both in God and in man intends the Kingdom of God, that is, the bringing of all things to creative dynamic harmony under the sovereign rule of God. Professor Niebuhr really accepts this: "The highest unity is a harmony of love in which the self relates itself in its freedom to other selves in their freedom under the will of God."[20] But if this be true where is the "ultimate contradiction" between the self-assertion of the human life and the divine *agape*?[21]

The Kingdom of God, let us say, is not the negation of any self, but rather the fulfillment of it. Therefore, *agape* intends a good which does include the ultimate good of the self. In intention universal mutual love and sacrificial love are one, for what is intended is the mutual good of all, and where this is really intended the self is ready to sacrifice anything for that good except the good itself. A formulation such as this is the only defense against a doctrine of love which involves the annihilation of the self. The difficulty which it involves in the Christian life must be faced in a moment. But here I want to point out that Niebuhr has not succeeded in bringing together his doctrine that sacrificial love is complete self-giving on the one hand, and his admission that the ultimate good involves the good of the self on the other.

This becomes quite clear in the case of a most interesting illustration which Niebuhr gives of the problem of the moral life. On the basis of his definition of *agape* he is forced to the conclusion:

... It is not even right to insist that every action of the Christian must conform to *agape*, rather than to the norms of relative justice and mutual love by which life is maintained and conflicting interests are arbitrated in history. For as soon as the life and interest of others than the agent are involved in an action or policy, the sacrifice of those interests ceases to be "self-sacrifice." It may actually become an unjust betrayal of their interests.[22]

This example reveals what is mistaken in Niebuhr's doctrine. He assumes that when I defend the interests of others my act can conform to *agape* in a sense which is impossible if I defend myself. But if the real good includes justice, then what difference *in principle* between defending justice for myself and justice for others? There is none. I say "in principle" because what Niebuhr is really pointing out is that when my own interests are involved the tendency to a corrupt assertion of those interests is very great, perhaps unavoid-

able in human life. It is not by any means clear, however, that even
this must be admitted without qualification.

Suppose a man belongs to an exploited group of workers. If he
organizes a union with the intent of creating the power which can
secure justice is he deficient in love because he recognizes himself
as a worker and intends that the justice which is won shall benefit
all workers including himself? On Niebuhr's view it would always
be impossible for the Christian to identify himself with the cause
for which he links his life with others, a curious conclusion. In this
connection Niebuhr's statement that Christ did not participate in
the claims and counterclaims of historical existence should be chal-
lenged. What of the defiance of the institution of the Sabbath? What
of the attack on the Pharisees? What of the blessing pronounced
upon the poor? These were assertions in history of what love intends
which had enormous practical consequences for historical institutions and powers. Even the saying, "Render unto Caesar the things
that are Caesar's and unto God the things that are God's," which has
indeed meant all things to all men, does assert that there are claims
which God makes in history. Since that statement was uttered the
political order has always found itself confronted by religious orders
which point to these claims and their consequences.

We said that in principle the good which *agape* seeks must include the good of the self, for the Kingdom of God does not exclude
any good, even my own. But the phrase "in principle" is important
because the question arises whether it is possible for this very human
flesh to include its own good in intention without corrupting it. It is
because Niebuhr sees the difficulty here and is able to point out
with such profound insight all the ways in which we deceive ourselves about our unselfishness that his work is of such inestimable
value. But the problem of sacrificial love is a practical problem of
the Christian life. What Niebuhr has done is to take the useful,
practical distinction between intending my own good and intending
the good of another without regard for self, and then to raise this

distinction to the level of a metaphysical dualism between sacrificial
and mutual love. St. Augustine is on sounder ground when he asserts that what we find in God is just our own true good for which
we were created.[23]

IV

These analyses point the way to a formulation of the idea of the
Kingdom of God which can be held without self-contradiction, and
which does offer a basis upon which the infinite variety and com-
plexity of moral and spiritual judgments can be made. In stating in
summary fashion the Christian conception of the Kingdom of God
we are not pretending that we can see perfectly what this means, nor
are we saying that we can arrive at a formal principle which can act
as a rule by which all Christian value judgments can be simply
made. Love is a spirit which overflows in a sense all static rules and
formal principles. What we can partially grasp in our Christian
experience is love's essential pattern, not its blueprint.[24]

The clue to our answer as to the nature of the good has already
been suggested. The love which is revealed in Christ is a love which
seeks the fulfillment of all things in such a relationship to one another that what flows from the life of each enriches the life of all,
and each participant in the whole life finds his own good realized
through the giving of self to the life of the whole. What may seem
abstract in formal statement is practical and clear in our common
experience. The fuller good resides where this life and that life, this
natural fact and that spiritual aspiration go together in such a way
that each person becomes more a whole person in serving the total
order of life actual and possible of which he is a part. Let us emphasize that this is an organic as over against a mechanical conception of the good. The rule of the greatest good for the greatest
number, for example, has a certain practical validity, but it implies
that the greater good can be arrived at by addition whereas our

principle points to the fact that the real good involves qualitative transformation of the order of life into a more subtle and complete mutual participation.

A universal community, then, in which each member is more free, more mature, more powerful through what he gives to and receives from every other member, is the best order we can think. It is the real good. It is the meaning of the Kingdom of God for human experience. The will to this community and the spirit in which we intend it and receive it is love.

We are speaking formally of the structure of the Kingdom of God. What this means concretely in all the uniqueness, variety, and infinite creativity of life, we can only faintly imagine and through experience patiently discover. It holds all the vast mystery of God within it and it stretches beyond our sight into the far reaches of time and eternity. But in the Christian experience of God's love in Christ, we have learned the secret of the Kingdom. We know what it means in human terms. It presses upon our human existence and we enter into it as God transforms our wills. How far the realization of the will to the Kingdom of God is possible for us is the question to which we must turn in the next chapter. We are recognizing here that in human experience we are not without a glimpse of the meaning of the Kingdom, and that in Christian experience we have seen its truth.

It remains to underline certain consequences of this Christian definition of the good. First as to the relation between mutual and sacrificial love. The good which the love of God intends is an order of mutuality. In His Kingdom all selves, all real values have their place. While each gives itself to the whole, each has its own claim upon the whole. For the good is just the good of each in the good of all. It is therefore not a denial of Christian love to intend my own good in the service of the Kingdom. That is the foundation of human struggles for freedom, justice, adequate material goods, more universal brotherhood. The Christian can intend nothing less than these, for they have their place in the Kingdom of God. The movement of redemption means nothing without them. The skillful mind and fingers of the surgeon who relieves human suffering, the plodding work of the politician who wades through the mud of political compromise to hold a city or a world together, the honest workmanship of the manual laborer or the creative artist— all of these are more indispensable to the Kingdom than the purest religious intention which will not stain itself with worldly action. According to St. Matthew's gospel Jesus accepts in the final judgment those who have fed the hungry and clothed the naked. This is no defense of the secular spirit. It is the assertion of the religious meaning of the secular life. As Dean Willard Sperry has said, "Christianity, thus interpreted, becomes not an added entity outside the major tasks of daily life, . . . but the sum of all particulars of unselfish and sacrificial service in the day's work, and an experience of actual community of sustaining spirit."[25]

The love which intends the mutuality of the Kingdom must become by that very intention sacrificial love, for the good is more than my good and the real good involves the giving of myself to the whole. Only a transformation of the human spirit into the willingness to give the self to the whole can suffice for the Kingdom. Here the pity and mystery of human sin shows itself. For I want to possess my good in myself alone. What is demanded of me is that nothing particular that I want for my own, even life, may be set against the claim of the Kingdom. The Christian sacrifice stands not on the basis of the simple altruistic formula of giving my life for others, but on the basis of so committing my life to the whole good of the Kingdom that nothing of my own shall stand in the way of this loyalty.

We can now see the sense in which the Christian view of the good involves the transvaluation of human values without negating them. Every judgment as to what is good must be made on the basis of what this particular concrete experience or action does for the movement of life toward the Kingdom. In the case of pleasure, for example, it is impossible to say whether pleasure is good or bad in itself. The question is what does this concrete particular pleasure do to the person who enjoys it, and to those whom his life touches. Kahlil Gibran says, "The lust for comfort murders the soul and then walks grinning in the funeral."[26] The higher virtues such as courage, temperance, however noble in themselves, still stand under the judgment of how in a particular life they serve or block the growth of the one universal good. The most refined religiousness can become God's most stubborn opposition as the conflict between Jesus and the Pharisees makes clear. Furthermore, it is true that suffering, pain, and conflict cannot be judged evil in themselves from the Christian point of view. They may serve to increase the sensitivity of the human spirit and to work its transformation into the spirit of love. Nowhere in life is the power of faith more apparent than in its capacity to make man face any experience, no matter what, with the hope that out of it some real good can come. This does not mean that no moral distinctions are to be made in life and that no experience should be avoided. There is evil—positive, destructive, violent. But any situation, no matter how riddled with evil, is subject to the creative transformation through which the human spirit is turned toward its true good.

We say man can be turned toward his true good, but is not that good always beyond? The transcendence of the Kingdom of God over the possibilities of this world consists partly in the obvious fact that the full realization of the whole order of mutuality is far from complete. But there is a deeper problem. In life as it is given to us to live, there seem to be permanent conditions which stand against the order of mutuality so that this world yearns for a good which in its very nature it cannot embody. Nature sets life against life. Human values split into a thousand varieties of incompatible ideals. We find ourselves divided by our very efforts to realize the wholeness of life. Berdyaev says that the creative life cannot aim at redemption. "Creative genius is not concerned with salvation or perdition. . . . If Pushkin went in for asceticism and sought the salvation of his soul, he would probably have ceased to be a great poet."[27] Professor Calhoun warns all sentimental humanitarians not to forget the "cruel puzzle" that truth-seeking and generosity can get man into trouble.[28] The human mind frequently seems to break down at the attempt to make valid practical judgments among the goods and evils of experience.

What we have tried to achieve so far is a statement of the meaning of the Kingdom. There is a goal of redemption which however vast and beyond our power to comprehend, still has an intelligible meaning in relation to our human values.

The attempt to define the good leads therefore to the question whether in any sense the order of complete mutuality is possible in this world. Is it possible for our very human flesh even to intend it? Can the love of God become the substance and the spirit of our life? To this question we now turn in an analysis of human society as it stands in relation to the Kingdom of God.

By arriving at this positive conclusion concerning the relation of self-realization in human life to the Kingdom of God we have not solved the problem of how far self-realization in the Kingdom of God is possible within human existence as we know it. Let us be clear about that. But by avoiding some of the errors in statements of this relationship which do violence to the nature of love we may prepare the way for a more reasoned judgment as to the possibility of this world's redemption. Love is to the Christian a term which points to an infinite holiness which always stands in judgment upon man, but the judgment is against man's sin, not against his existence as a man.

CHAPTER FOUR

The Kingdom of God and the Kingdoms of This World

ONE petition in the Lord's Prayer gathers up our human need and our Christian hope: "Thy kingdom come, thy will be done on earth as it is in heaven." This prayer is the Christian's lever to move the world.

Liberal Christianity had faith that the world can be moved. The Kingdom it believed is coming in history. World-bettering is Kingdom-building. He who shares in that work knows that his life is linked with the purpose of God. Every victory of righteousness moves the whole creation toward its consummation in the everlasting community of love.

Today the conviction is growing among Christians of many different theological persuasions that we can no longer hold to this interpretation of the coming of the Kingdom on earth. The abyss between the Kingdom of God and the kingdoms of this world has opened up before our eyes. We are perplexed to know what to make of our tragic world history, and to know how as Christians we are to live in it.

We must examine the roots of this perplexity, and show why its solution lies in an interpretation of the creative and redemptive work of God which is other than that of either liberalism or neo-orthodoxy. Our attention is now directed to a problem where perplexity is perhaps greatest, the relation of the Christian ideal of the good to the realities of the political order. All the social problems have in our time taken on a "political" dimension. Witness how

economics now has become again "political economy." The problem of Christian ethics in politics is especially urgent. If we can find
the signs of the Kingdom of God in politics, we can doubtless find
them anywhere!

I

The very phrase "power politics" seems to exclude every moral
consideration, let alone a Christian ideal of life. The struggle for
world law and order has enlisted the mind and devotion of men of
good will. They have had few more forceful spokesmen than Mr.
E. B. White whose editorials in the *New Yorker,* published under
the title of "The Wild Flag," put the case for world government
with unsurpassed clarity and with a seasoning of humor which
makes them far more effective than dry solemnity. Examine these
sentences from the public letter which Mr. White addressed to the
American delegates at the opening of the United Nations:

> When you sit down, sit down as an American if it makes you feel com-
> fortable, but when you rise to speak, get up like a man anywhere. . . .
> Bear in mind always that foreign policy is domestic policy with its hat
> on. The purpose of the meeting . . . is to replace policy with law, and to
> make common cause.
> Think not to represent us by safeguarding our interests. Represent us by
> perceiving that our interests are other people's and theirs ours.
> Be concerned with principles, not with results. We do not ask for results,
> merely for a soil-building program. You are not at a chess game, even
> though it has the appearance of one, you are at a carnival of hope.
> Build the great republic.[1]

Beneath the urbane surface of these words we cannot fail to hear
the authentic accents of moral faith and human good sense. Yet,
irresistible as they are, they plunge us into every problem of the
political order. The delegates are appealed to as individuals, yet we
know they must act under compulsions and orders which are determined by all kinds of political stakes and decisions at home. They

are urged to recognize the harmony of interests of all nations, yet as the political scientist E. H. Carr has pointed out, it is the collapse of belief in the harmony of interests which constitutes the crisis in economic and political theory today.[2] Mr. White pleads that we replace the search for isolated security of one nation with devotion to the common cause of all. But can a nation do that? Is it not the case that nations are in their very nature fated to throw themselves at one another in a grim game of power to which the principles of ethics are no more relevant than to the death battle of prehistoric mastodons? Finally, Mr. White puts his faith in an order of law as the substitute for rule by conflict of powers. But have we not had to learn that law reflects and in large part depends upon the power structure of society? The dictum that "the Sermon on the Mount is not for statesmen," has become a predominant influence upon Christian political theory in our time.[3] One contemporary Christian philosopher rejects all naïve ethical idealism in politics with the assertion: "The Christian kingdom is not of this world, it belongs to the realm of the spirit. In this world, it is always Caesar who is bound to be victorious, while Christ will for ever be crucified."[4]

No one can doubt that the crisis for the liberal Christian interpretation of politics is very great. Liberalism put hope largely in the possibility of creating the good state in which force would be either unnecessary, or would function only as police power under law. But the actual forces in society are always partially at least anarchic and ruthless. The theological ethics of neo-orthodoxy must be understood as an attempt to achieve responsible Christian action in the political sphere, but to do this in the face of the contradiction between that order and the demands of love.

We must bear in mind what the real question we must answer is. It is not the question whether our social and political life is now what it ought to be; nor even whether it is better than other social orders have been. The problem is not perfection in politics. We may very well believe, though it is debatable, that injustice and violence are worse in our century than in any previous time. But the question is: Are there certain unchangeable facts in the human situation which compel us to recognize that the contradiction between the Kingdom of God and the kingdoms of this world is ineradicably present in life itself? Neo-orthodoxy says there are such facts; liberalism denies it. I shall try to show that there is an answer which differs from both of these.

II

The whole neo-orthodox case against the liberal doctrine that the orders of this world can be transformed into the Kingdom of love rests ultimately on two propositions about the actual situation of man in nature and in society, which we need carefully to examine. These propositions are held to be universally applicable to all men's life, but they have special relevance to the political order. One of these is that human history is the arena of competitive power, and that therefore it contradicts in its essence the order of love. The other is that all human relations are caught in impersonal orders which contradict the spirit of Christian love which is wholly personal. We shall examine the problem of power and conflict in Reinhold Niebuhr's thought, for he stresses it most; and the problem of personality and the impersonal in the work of Emil Brunner who makes it his basic concept.

There are moralists who hold that all actual historical power is evil. In the last century Jacob Burckhardt said, "Power is in itself evil."[5] Today Professor Hans Morgenthau says that the "ubiquity of the desire for power . . . constitutes the ubiquity of evil in human action."[6] Hence, he concludes "to the degree to which the essence and aim of politics is power over man, politics is evil." But politics "is a struggle for power over men." The conclusion is unavoidable, "political ethics is indeed the ethics of doing evil."[7] Professor Carr leans toward the same position when he speaks of "that uneasy compromise between power and morality which is the foundation of all political life," thus implying that power is the factor which compromises morality.[8]

It is instructive that Niebuhr never quite allows himself to fall into this flat equation of power with evil. There are good reasons in the Christian faith why he does not; for God is both goodness and power. He has created this world of creatures with their particular powers, and has created them good.[9] Niebuhr therefore says explicitly: "Power is not evil of itself."[10] But while he thus appears to lay the foundation for a view of ethics which gives a positive place to power, the judgment to which we are forced to come, I think, is that in effect Niebuhr's position finally amounts to saying that all historical vitalities and power are *actually* in contradiction to the demand of love.

How it is possible for him to come to this conclusion is seen if we analyze Niebuhr's doctrine of sin. He believes that in the human situation we are inevitably involved in the sins of pride and self-assertion. How in this case man can be said to be free is one of the paradoxes which Niebuhr holds defies rational understanding.[11] But if we accept the paradox, while we may say there is an *ideal* possibility that we could assert our human will to power in history without sinning and thus bring in the Kingdom of love, this is no *actual* possibility. Actually our will to power is asserted as a sinful egoism. Now in a world of competing egos conflict is inevitable. And Niebuhr holds that conflict is always evil. He remarks that "Nietzschean morality perversely transposes all values and raises the disease of social life, conflict, to the eminence of the criterion of all values"[12] Conflict within the self or between selves is always evil. Thus for Niebuhr all self-assertion of individual or group in history contradicts the demands of the Gospel, and involves us in the sinful warfare of interests. Since there is no escape from self-assertion in human life, there is no escape from conflict, nor from coercion which is covert conflict. And both are evil.

We are here at the most crucial point of all Christian ethics, and of the Christian world view itself. What has happened in Niebuhr's theology, and in the whole movement of neo-orthodoxy is this: It has taken two truths which it has asserted against liberalism and has drawn a false conclusion from them. One truth is that a philosophy such as Nietzsche's which glorifies conflict and coercion can and has been used to justify terrible and destructive evil. The other truth is that in all human conflict there is probably an element of sinful misuse of freedom and of self-assertion at the expense of the real good. But the erroneous conclusion is drawn that *all* conflict and coercion, *all* historical assertion of power, is actually in itself evil.

This conclusion does not follow. It can be shown to be false. Consequently we can see what it is in neo-orthodoxy which separates the Kingdom of God too completely from the kingdoms of this world; and we can see what it is that is lacking in its appreciation of the goodness of life.

Power is essential to life. To be anything is to possess some power of one's own and to assert it. But, more important, the *conflict* of powers, of interests, of life with life can and does function constructively in the growth and good of life. The glorification of conflict within the self, or between life and life may, to be sure, become the justification of appalling evil or it may sink into a sentimental romanticism which has nothing to do with the goal of Christian aspiration. But what we have to see is that there is a perfectly natural and useful friction of life with life, of interest with interest, of will with will. Seriously, now, who would want to live in a world where there was no clash, no friction, no contest of ideas or of spirit?

Consider the matter of coercion, in relation to the growth of personality. Coercion in the home certainly means that there is some conflict between the immediate desire and will of a child and his parents, and the exercises of coercion by a parent perhaps always produces some conflict in the child. Yet the growth of personality is impossible without this element. Dr. Hocking puts the logic clearly: "In the course of nature, human beings arrive at self-government by way of a long regime of parental coercion. The presence of coercion, therefore, cannot be incompatible with the growth of spontaneous lawfulness."[13] This is not to deny what Niebuhr and others have shown of the subtle ways in which sin may be expressed in the tyrannies of parents over children. A counselor tells of the girl who reported, "Father always lets us have his way." But the evil is in the tyranny, not in the coercion. In some human relations at least coercion is not only necessary, which Niebuhr of course admits, but also it is an essential element in the growth of the real good of mutuality among free and responsible persons.[14]

But what of overt conflict? Is that not always evil? Let us take one example of the way in which conflict may serve the good of life which has been sadly neglected. Professor Frank Knight is right in saying that philosophers and theologians have paid far too little attention to play.[15] Some play involves competitive games. The game has its competitors each striving to win, its testing in a fair field, and the deeper testing in the bearing of victory and defeat. A great part of the zest and worth of play depends on the element of conflict which it holds. Where there is no will to win on both sides there is no real game.

It may be objected that this reference to play proves the point of the evil in real conflict; for it might be argued that the essence of play is that the conflict is not quite real. The normal demands of life are relaxed. We can afford the luxury of the contest in which no one really gets hurt, and in which the value of enjoyment is secured to all participants in spite of the outcome. But let us consider the possibility that the acceptance of conflict, in the spirit of play— that is, with the will to see it through—has a far broader and deeper role in life. The very zest of life itself depends partly on the fact that as individuals and as groups we have to find our way to one another and to make terms with one another through the friction of wills and interests. We need the willingness to accept the friction as a necessary part of the way toward mature living together.

The principle that conflict is essential to the wholesome growth of mutuality in human relations can be directly applied to our understanding of one aspect of politics which theologians have too often neglected. Mr. T. V. Smith, professor and politician, has caught the spirit of American politics with a human understanding which reveals how it is possible to discover the creative element in political conflict. Professor Smith believes that democracy has discovered one of the foundations of human good in what he calls the "legislative way of life." That way of life, he says frankly, is "built upon conflict"; but the state of mind essential to it is one which holds competition among ideas, ideals, and persons to be itself a standard and fruitful form of co-operation.[16] A veteran of Chicago politics once tried to explain the fascination the career held for him: "I kept at it because it was recreation to me. I always like a good fight; the chance, the suspense, interest me. I never gambled nor played cards so it was fun to me."[17] Now one may find something less than the pure spirit of love here but there is also disclosed a valuable element in human nature which a Christian ethic ought to respect and enlist, not relegate to a place wholly outside the Kingdom.

T. V. Smith links the ideal of sportsmanship to the spirit of a wholesome political activity.[18] He suggests that this sportsmanship involves a certain humility. Where I do not admit that my opponent may have any truth in him at all I no longer really compete with him. I find ways to deny him the right to compete. Democracy as an ideal might be said to be the attempt to accord to every person the possibility of finding his rightful share in the social good through an order in which his interests and claims will have a fair hearing, and through a political process in which whatever power he can legitimately muster will be able to make itself felt. It is a long way from such an ideal of political activity to the actualities in which it is carried on; but it is essential to our human attempt to

live together to see that the "game of politics" is not merely a necessary evil but that it has at its best a link with legitimate good.

This point may be reinforced by one further consideration. Conflict has its dangers, its risks, its destructive forms, and its way of
corrupting the human spirit. But it is equally true that harmony, at
the biological, psychological, and social levels, also has its risks and
its evils. We are seeking the real good of human life under the conditions imposed by our world. It seems clear that tension, friction,
the moving of mind against mind and will against will, are our
protection against stagnation. The exaltation of integration as the
psychological ideal appears to overlook this simple truth. The best
integrated persons are rarely the most sensitive, useful, or creative
even in dealing with their own problems. I quote Dr. Hocking again
in his keen observation on the function of anger: "The reflective
awareness of anger contains the perception that conflict, instead of
being the purely disintegrating force we commonly regard it, has a
constructive function; that it is a process which associate life
normally goes through on its way to more durable foundations."[19]
Consider in this connection the observation of a psychiatrist that
the only completely happy people are the hopeless cases who have
surrendered every tension and are in complete self-satisfaction. The
implications of this view of conflict for the problem of the economic
order we shall examine later; but we may remark here that even
contemporary socialist economic theory has made a place for types
of competition among producing units within the co-operative
society.[20]

Though we argue that it is far too simple to say that the conflict
of wills among men contradicts their real good, let us be clear that
it is far too simple to say that conflict is necessarily good. I am plead-
ing for no Social Darwinism nor for a Nietzschean view of human
society. Neither am I arguing that all conflict ultimately serves the
good through God's Providence. Hegel's idealism is a mistaken
simplification of the problem of evil when he says, "This process or

course of finitude, of pain, strife, victory, is a moment or stage in the nature of Spirit."[21] There is real evil which destroys spirit, and much of it takes the form of destructive conflict. The conclusion of our analysis is that Christian ethics ought to make most careful discrimination as to types of conflict and of harmony, and set forth the conditions under which both conflict and harmony may serve and those under which they may block the growth of mutuality. War, for example, is one type of conflict, and it seems clear that modern war involves such wholesale destruction that the most one can say is that its outcome may prevent worse evil, not that it serves any positive good. But all conflict is not warfare, nor does it involve violent destruction of the opponent. A recent commentator on labor problems says, "Collective bargaining is civil war." It may be that, but it may also be the place where for the first time the worker and his employer meet with such balance of power that each is forced to listen to the position of the other.[22] Some employers have been won over to the collective bargaining method through the discovery that they could learn more about efficient production through this process.[23]

If the preceding argument be sound we have found the creative goodness of God at a place where theologians have forgotten to look for it. When Niebuhr describes life as "a welter of perils and passions"[24] one may accept his description as essentially true. But there is a work of God in the midst of this dark reality which brings forth matured, self-reliant, free persons whose freedom has been nurtured by their participation in that friction of will against will which makes up so much of life. Passion, contention, peril, and adventure belong to the goodness of life as much as to its evil. They are "the terms of mortal life";[25] and a just Christian appreciation of them will recognize even in the darker patterns of life the weaving of the creative hand of God.

Now it is clear why we can say that God's good is revealed *in* history, not only at the edge of it. Niebuhr's argument that the revelation in Christ takes place only at the edge of history is based on the doctrine that all conflict of power is evil. History is the field of competing powers. Therefore Christ "refuses to participate in the claims and counter-claims of historical existence."[26] That as we have already observed surely is in flat contradiction to the record. Jesus denounced the Pharisees, a social and religious elite, for laying heavy burdens on the poor. He broke with the institution of the sabbath which was deeply entwined with the social, economic, and religious life of the Jewish people. He healed the sick. He gathered a group of disciples and sent them out to teach. His teaching so threatened the political and ecclesiastical powers that they destroyed him. The consequence, whether intended or unintended, of his life was the formation of the Church whose existence is a part of the very fabric of all Western social and political history since its beginning. If all this is not exercising power in history it is hard to see what to make of it.

It is true that the ultimate problem of the relation of the ethic of love to the relativities of the political orders cannot be simply solved. But what we have established so far is that the exercise of power in history, the expression of the interests, vitalities, and wills which belong to us as human beings, and even the participation in the inevitable conflict of these interests and vitalities, are not in contradiction to the real human good which is the earthly content of our life in the love of God. The Kingdom of God has a purchase upon the kingdoms of this world which liberalism conceived too simply but which its critics have only faintly recognized.

III

As we turn now to the problem of the Kingdom and the political order as put by Emil Brunner in his great work, *The Divine Imperative*, we note that the same argument we have examined in Niebuhr appears also in Brunner. He describes the demand of love as a pure ideal standing against all coercion and conflict. Hence the state, which wields the sword, imprisons and executes the criminal, must obey a different law from that of love.

> By force of compulsion the individual State gains respect from other states, and by force of compulsion it maintains its unity over against the opposing will of individuals and of groups. It is by this that the action of the State is a contradiction of the law of love; it is this which makes it a moral problem. In itself compulsion is contrary to love; it is sinful.[27]

We must live and act as Christians in this order of the state as also we must live in the economic order, and in the family, but "we should be fully aware that the Christian, in the service of love, is summoned to place himself within an order which is inherently loveless."[28]

If we ask where this inherent break between the necessary conditions of social life and the command to love our neighbor occurs we find a new argument in Brunner. He holds that the Christian ethic of love is a purely personal ethic and can therefore be realized only in a person-to-person relationship which is never wholly possible in this world. He says the ethos of institutions and systems is always different from the ethos of *agape*. Justice is the rule in institutions and "justice belongs," says Brunner, "to the world of systems, not to the world of persons. . . . Within the system as such there can be nothing higher, for love knows nought of systems."[29]

Brunner's thought here shows the influence of a book which has rightly exercised on contemporary thought, an influence all out of proportion to its length, Martin Buber's *I and Thou*.[30] Buber, the Jewish philosopher and mystic, has given a fresh interpretation to the religious problem. He sees our human world divided into two primary dimensions, the personal dimension of I and Thou, and the impersonal dimension of I and It. Impersonal relations are governed by calculations of use. I recognize whatever I find myself related to merely as an impersonal thing. "It" may be my employee, my student, or anything which is the object of my rational calculation. I try to bring the other into the service of my ego. In the personal relationships all this disappears and two subjects are face to face, not to use each other nor to seek domination, but in the freedom and community of love.

Buber's profound expression of the yearning for the full reality of personal existence possesses great power because it hits straight at the primary need of our society. The spiritual struggle of Western man can be interpreted as his search for a way of life which will make possible free personal selfhood in the midst of all the forces, dogmatic, ecclesiastical, economic, social, and technical, which depersonalize him. When, on the wall of a labor union head-quarters, we read, "Love thy neighbor, but organize him," we see the necessity; yet we instinctively sense the threat that every organiza-tion, labor unions no more than any other, makes to the free per-sonal relationship. Every judge faces this when he is confronted with the conflict between the impartial demands of the law and the actual personal needs of those before the law. All of us fret and kick against the steel bands of institutionalism; the teacher against the grading system, the social worker against the artificiality created by the very fact of his being a professional representative of the state commissioned to deal with human needs, the worker something of whose very life is "bought" against the employer, and the sensitive employer who buys that portion of that life against the system, the public official against the role which political necessity assigns to him. A Jewish proverb says, "When a man is appointed an official on earth, he becomes a man of evil above."[31] Martin Luther writing on secular authority cautiously observed, "It is not impossible for a prince to be a Christian though it is a rare thing and surrounded with difficulties."[32]

Institutionalism is only one aspect of the problem. There is the whole influence of scientific calculation on the human mind and spirit. There is the vastness of the economic and political powers which toss individuals about as chips. There is the flood of standard-

ized amusement, reading, radio, all of which produces a kind of
dumb mass-mindedness. The very glorification of the strong individual, and the hysterical emotion centered upon "personalities
in the news," reflects the feeble hold which we have on our own
selfhood.[33] How desperately we search for that personal reality which
will vicariously, if not directly, help us to feel we possess our own
hearts and will. Martin Buber and Emil Brunner, Max Weber and
Nicolas Berdyaev have penetrated to this real inner crisis in the
modern spirit.

But consider now Brunner's view of the consequence of this
analysis for Christian ethics. We know we have to live in institutions,
orders, and under laws. How are we to be guided in these areas
where *agape* is shattered by impersonality?

Brunner's answer is that where we cannot express love directly we
must be guided by the ethics of rational ideas, of calculations, of
adjustment of means to ends. Justice and equality are rational
ideals. They "do not know love."[34] "Love strides over all man-made
barriers, brushes aside the 'claims of equity,' and presses forward to
meet the other."[35] "Legalism is the evil."[36] "The legalistic type of
person finds it impossible to come into real human, personal contact
with his fellow-man."[37] He sums up, "These orders do not obey the
logic of faith or of love, but the logic of the human and the rational
positing of an end."[38] "There certainly is an insoluble dualism
between the law of the orders and the commandment of love."[39]

Now there is a warning signal in such statements which ought to
put us on our guard. We are encountering the same error which we
discovered in Niebuhr. Something which belongs to the necessary
good of human life, in this case the rational guidance of life by
critical evaluation of means and ends, is asserted to be in contradiction to the demand of love. What has become of the Christian
doctrine that man is created in the image of God? Where is the
recognition that the necessities of our human life serve love and do
not always destroy it?

Brunner's answer is that this legalistic element enters into life not through the creation itself but through sin. The universal necessity for rational ethical calculation within the orders is a consequence of original sin. In effect, then, just as he and Niebuhr conclude that conflict contradicts love, Brunner concludes that all law contradicts love. This I believe we must reject as a serious distortion of the Christian view of life and of Christian ethics. It is a half-truth, not a whole-truth.

Certainly the Christian ethic is a personal ethic. Its aim is a so-ciety of free and responsible individuals, with the life of each made more full and more free through sharing in the life of all. But we must not overlook the fact that in human life the growth of whole-some personal relations depends in part on the existence of certain impersonal elements. The impersonal factors in laws and institu-tions and rational ethical principles are not merely concessions to sin. They enter into and support the growth of the personal factors. We miss the wonder of human personality if we look for it solely in the factors of consciousness and mentality and moral freedom. The most wonderful thing is that these factors appear within and are co-ordinated through the vast world of structures and processes which are not personal. It is the creative work of God which achieves in personality a unique organization of impersonal struc-tures which becomes a new center of power and direction reacting upon the impersonal order. A. N. Whitehead's metaphysical insight here undergirds the alternative to the personalism of Brunner and Buber. For Whitehead, "though life in its essence is the gain of intensity through freedom, yet it can also submit to canalization and so gain the massiveness of order."[40]

For illustration of the importance of this order to personality con-sider the significance of privacy in personal relationships. It is a strange thing, this business of the locked door, the fence, the prayer in secret, the retreats which we make from one another. We are rightly uneasy about it all for there probably always creeps into our isolation a sinful element. Yet there is something more to be said. The retreat of privacy, of physical and psychical freedom from the other, is imperative for the healthy growth of personality even in the most intimate human relationships. Those who know the effects on human personality of the tragic overcrowding which goes with poverty and poor housing continually remind us that this means children grow up "without privacy." They are exposed to all the experiences of adult life before they are ready to interpret them; and the consequences on personality may be damaging beyond repair.

Every person needs the protection of his own growing feeling and insight against the ruthless and inopportune invasion of another. Jacques Barzun rightly objects to the prevalence of the custom of demanding of applicants for admission to schools that they state in full their good intentions and purposes in making the move. "No human being," he says, "should be asked to display worthy motives on request."[41] We cannot achieve the deeper levels of personal friendship except by respecting that barrier of privacy without which the slow and delicate growth of understanding will be killed. I venture that this may be the reason why in general men achieve in their friendships a greater success than do women. Men maintain personal loyalty without insisting on intruding into that which the other does not care to reveal. Women in our culture are less secure in their friendship, and they cannot stand the possibility that the other "may have secrets." This necessary distance in personal relations does not prove that we are sinners under the curse of an angry God. It proves that we are human beings under the limitations of finite existence. It is a dangerous sentimentality to exalt a pure and unmediated meeting of subjects in the I-Thou relationship as the only true good.

To the function of privacy must be added the function of impersonal principle in the philosophy of personal relations. We have already pointed out that the world largely consists of subpersonal processes and abstract structures as we encounter it. But the discovery of this impersonal character of the setting of our life does not destroy personality. It offers the enduring order in which personality can exist. The discovery of common structures and principles which stand impartially beyond the particular wishes and passions of individuals offers that stable common ground in which we can begin to achieve social existence. The most important application of this truth to our present problem is the conclusion that the search for rational ethical order is not a contradiction of Christian love. The discovery of ethical principle is the first step in the achievement of the full dignity and meaning of personal existence. That God is both love and law is the doctrine of the whole Judeo-Christian tradition. The discovery of the rational order which makes intelligible our being and our moral life is one of the first steps in our discovery that we live and move and have our being in God. Our lives are embraced by a universal intelligible order which makes possible a human social existence in which something beyond arbitrary whim and power is operative.

It is therefore too simple a judgment that the law of the state, enforced by power, always contradicts the ethic of love. Law provides one of the conditions of personal freedom when it imposes an element of impersonal principle upon all the members of the society. It offers the stable order and the articulation of principle by which men can live together in moral relationships.

There is to be sure something in the spirit of love which overflows all abstract principle. But our point is that the spirit needs the undergirding structure of law for its own development. Emil Brunner seems to admit this when he says that God has given us the "orders" of the family, state, etc., for the sake of our education in community. But if they perform this function how are they so alien to that love which is the heart of the Christian ethic? When, for example, we try to define the rights of men in the political order, we are to be sure setting up legal fences between persons. We are not creating love. We are saying what personal freedoms shall not be violated on pain of punishment. But at the same time we are designating certain ways of life, and giving them collective sanction which are entitled to the loyalty of all members of the society regardless of private wishes or convenience. The state which establishes freedom of speech in its constitution and enforces it has added a necessary element to the spiritual as well as to the political basis of the common life.

Let us readily admit that no problem of modern life is more profound than that of saving personality from destruction amidst the titanic powers released in a technological civilization. But the solution of that problem in so far as we can conceive it has a quite different emphasis from that implied by Brunner's analysis. The key is not to view the institutionalization of life, the extension of legal controls, and the multiplication of collective political structures as something in itself alien to the Christian ideal of love; rather, it is to discover the kind of political conditions under which the growth of love can be furthered.

One application of this conception of the place of personality in the social order is of so great importance for the present crisis in Christian thought that we should take special account of it. This is the problem of the Christian attitude toward the positive law of the state. Both liberal political philosophy and liberal Christianity have put a large measure of trust in the achievement of the good society through establishment of a legal constitutional order which embodies the essential ideals of justice and equality. We are now in a period of serious questioning of how far that faith was justified. Certainly there are grave limitations. Law in itself does not "make people good." The actual law of any state must be recognized as depending upon the complex of powers and interests which establish it and upon which its enforcement depends. Every particular law will represent in part the temporary achievement of a balance or compromise between conflicting interests. It will be something less

than perfect justice. Law can never enact mutuality. But what is not
to be forgotten is that while law "reflects" the community, law also
becomes a creative element in the mind and will of the community.
Law is a social psychological fact as well as a political fact. It is a
means by which a people may educate and discipline its own spirit
for better or for worse.

An American experiment in the function of law in racial relations
is now being carried out. Not only are laws which segregate races
being attacked, but positive laws which make it a crime to spread
racial prejudice are being passed. Through fair employment prac-
tices acts some states are seeking to outlaw discrimination in employment based on racial or creedal background. The successful
experience of the State of New York with such a law in which hun-
dreds of cases have been adjusted satisfactorily even without recourse to the courts encourages us to believe that the difficulties are
not nearly so great as some feared or wanted us to believe.[42] It is true
that one can easily put too much faith in sheer legislation which
may be rendered futile if it is not supported in the community consciousness. But the significance of such a law is not only that it puts
the coercive power of the state against the unjust discriminator, but
that it puts the moral power of the state against it also. T. V. Smith's
statement that laws "represent the maximum of private conscience
which can at any time become social fact," applies to be sure only
where law is created not by some arbitrary decree but by a process
which can reflect the public mind.[43] But where this process exists,
the man who finds the law lying across his path is confronted not
only with a political power but with a moral judgment. In the FEP
laws and Civil Rights Act of 1964 there is an implied judgment
that discrimination is morally wrong. Individuals may or may not
agree with this judgment; but its very existence in the form of law
is a social fact putting the weight of the collective conscience behind a positive conception of the rights of men.

The liberal faith that law can positively serve the good is not naïve. What is really naïve is to fail to see that law operates dynamically in the consciousness of the community. This has been abundantly proved in the history of the law of race relations in America.

Carey McWilliams points out the use which was made of the laws discriminating against property holding by Japanese in California. These began with one school board which adopted ordinances segregating Oriental students. Agitation for anti-Oriental laws was continued by labor leaders who were welding a political labor movement. McWilliams concludes:

Anti-Oriental prejudice became a part of the mores in large part as a result of incessant propaganda and agitation for the enactment of various legislative proposals. . . . It would also seem that legislative pattern of discrimination once achieved, tended to function as a means by which these same attitudes were kept alive.[44]

McWilliams quotes from Justice Harlan's dissent in a famous civil rights case in the Supreme Court, Plessy vs. Ferguson, which puts the point with classic simplicity:

What can more certainly arouse race hate, what more certainly create and perpetuate a feeling of distrust between these races than state enactments which, in fact, proceed upon the grounds that colored citizens are so inferior and degraded that they cannot be allowed to sit in public coaches occupied by white citizens?[45]

We can see now why we cannot accept Brunner's statement that the state "cannot itself be creative."[46] The state is always creative for good or evil. It not only reflects but it helps to produce the mind and spirit of the community. Liberal Christianity was right in finding a place for the direct expression of Christian love in politics, for politics is statecraft. The administrator, legislator, statesman, or ward chairman who works at his task in pursuit of the creation of an order of life in which the full dignity and freedom of men can be realized is expressing Christian love as truly as it can be expressed anywhere. We can admit that to say "love thy neighbor, but organize him" poses difficulties; but we do not need to surrender the conviction that the responsible organization of power for the ends of human justice and freedom is a true expression of Christian love.

In the State of Colorado in 1944 a special session of the legislature was called to consider a bill to outlaw the holding of property by all persons of Japanese origin. It appeared to have a chance of being passed. In the first hours of the debate a legislator named Hill, so recently discharged from the army he was still in uniform, spoke against the bill. He had been warned that he was committing political suicide but he said: "I am just as willing to die a political death as I am to die in battle to preserve American freedom."[47] After that, the reporter says, the campaign "sputtered and went out like a wet fuse." The word which makes the difference between good and evil in a political controversy can be spoken. The spirit which seeks the real good lives a precarious life in the world of snarling predatory interests; but it lives.

The service of God in our time is in part a responsible participation in the political order, and in part the creation of an international political order. That is not merely idealism; it is Christian realism. The conditions of human life with all the conflict, the grasping for power, the institutionalism are not in hopeless contradiction to the order which can open the way to the greatest human good. A Christian theology which recognizes this will sustain the effort to create the foundations of that order.

IV

What vision of God's creative and redemptive work in history emerges from this analysis? Do we mean to identify such human works as the creation of justice through the state with the activity of God? I suggest we do not need to make such an identification and we should not. Human activity we can understand as having the possibility of providing conditions under which the work of grace may be more fully released. We can go further and say that under human limitations we can mediate the grace of God through the spirit and activities of resistance to evil, of mercy and reconciliation in the human community. But we must acknowledge that God's work itself is always something more than our works; and in its full depth and power and wholeness stands in judgment over our human working.

On this vital doctrine that the grace of God is operative in our human history we stand with the liberal theology. The error of neo-orthodoxy in its various forms can now be summarily stated. As we have seen in both Niebuhr and Brunner, there is a failure to recognize the creative work of God because there is a false doctrine of original sin which leads to a false appraisal of the natural conditions of human life. Both Niebuhr and Brunner affirm the need and the reality of redemption. Here too the interpretation of original sin works its unfortunate consequences; for now redemption is no longer an actual transformation of life; it is primarily sheer forgiveness of sin and the promise of an ultimate reconciliation beyond history. That this is somewhat qualified by both Niebuhr and Brunner, I recognize; but that is the tendency of their position.

Specifically then we have every right to regard the political order as having the potentiality of serving both the creative and the redemptive work of God. The state may provide some of the conditions of mutuality in the common life. The state knows something of mercy; for no civilized penal code is without its gesture toward the possible restoration of the wrongdoer to society. A wise public official after observing politics in an American city for a number of years said that he would prefer having the city run by elected officials with all the dangers which that involves to administration by political experts; for the politicians often have a human kindness and mercy which the experts lack. It was the chief of state at the end of the Civil War who said, "With malice toward none; with charity for all." Should those words have been reserved for the pulpit? Were they out of place in politics?

Two misunderstandings should be avoided. First, in declaring that the grace of reconciliation moves through the political order, however tenuous its hold there, we must avoid the error of identifying the political order with the whole of the human community. MacIver rightly points out that this identification is an idealistic error which leads to totalitarian deification of the state. The community is more than the state.[48] The creative and redemptive work of God we may readily admit depends perhaps more basically upon the voluntary associations, the communities of artists, the scientists, and the schools than upon the political order. Thoreau remarks that "all the abuses which are the objects of reform are unconsciously amended in the intercourse of friends."[49] A labor union which brings new dignity to the lives of its members and which creates good will among racial groups, a corporation which pioneers in the field of securing a more just system of labor relationships, a school system which brings brotherhood not only into its classroom but into the lives of the students and their families, a group of scientists who give time and effort to seeking the establishment of a rational and effective control over atomic energy, all this can be the human service of the creative and redemptive work of God.

Secondly, the Church has a special relationship to the grace of God. It is founded on the love and mercy of God who has through Jesus Christ created this community as the human bearer of His spirit in history. The Church as a universal community of freedom and fellowship makes possible the reconciliation of man with God and his fellows in a way which no other historical community can accomplish. The Church is not the only channel of God's grace, though understood in its full meaning it is the most important one.

If we now can go this far in discovering within the actual orders of our life the saving work of God we may seem to be returning to the liberal interpretation of the coming of the Kingdom of God on earth. If in spite of all evil the grace of God is present with power in history, why can we not believe that the long trend of history is toward the achievement of that perfected life which is the earthly counterpart of the Kingdom of God for whose coming we pray? There is a strong temptation to accept "a long run optimism" in which we conceive of sin and evil as being progressively eliminated.

But this temptation must be resisted. If we reject the Christian pessimism of neo-orthodoxy, we must also reject this formula of liberal optimism. The reasons why this is so, and the interpretation of history to which we are led, will be examined.

CHAPTER FIVE

Time, Progress, and the Kingdom of God

THE Christian faith that God works creatively and redemptively in human history does not contradict the facts of history. It is required by those facts when we see deeply enough into them. So we have asserted. We have argued that man's bond with the ultimate structure of God's good, and man's dependence upon the working of God's power is disclosed in the midst of the turmoil of our existence. We can discern the presence of the ultimate order of love even in the political orders where compromise, clash of interests, and warfare seem to prevail in disregard of the divine law. God's Kingdom, which is the assertion of His love with power, does "press upon" the world at every moment. Yet even as we make this assertion we recognize that we live in actual estrangement from God. There is a dark reality of evil which sets the creation against God's love, and turns the human heart upon itself. We are left therefore with the perplexity which we must examine in this chapter. Can we believe in the progress of the reign of God in history or is the ultimate conflict between His Kingdom and the kingdoms of this world unresolved to the end of time?

I

The question of progress involves the problem of the nature of time which has been hovering on the edge of our discussion and which must now be brought to the center of attention. Our life passes from birth to death. The world moves into its future, and moment by moment dies away. What is lost and what is saved in this everlasting passage? Does God's Kingdom really grow in depth and fulfillment through the long sweep of the ages, or is that merely an outworn liberal notion which has brought liberal theology to its present extremity?

There are some who say that all attempts to speak of the course of events in relation to an indeterminate future are speculative and fruitless. Had we not better say "it doth not yet appear what we shall be" and go about our business unafraid and untroubled? Certainly humility and reserve are appropriate. No questions lead us so quickly beyond our depth as those concerning time. There is a certain practical wisdom in refusing to allow the fulfillment of today's task to depend upon answers to obscure questions about tomorrow.

Yet to leave the matter there is not only superficial, it is paralyzing to action, for hope has practical consequences. Hope in the human spirit means its relation to the future before it, the eternity above it, and the saving of the precious values of its past. The depth and range of hope qualifies our sense of the worth of the present. I am in part what I hope for; for what I am is what I am willing to commit myself to, and that depends upon what I believe finally counts. As Professor Whitehead observes, "The greater part of morality hinges upon relevance in the future."[1] I encounter my neighbor as one who shares with me the fate of death. If death destroys for me my hope, it also destroys my valuation of my neighbor. I can treat him as a bit of earth dust, to be exploited for whatever momentary benefit I can secure from him. But if my hope for all of life involves the belief that the good of life has eternal stature then I see my neighbor in a different light. Berdyaev is profoundly right in insisting that all ethics needs eschatology.[2] One factor in the sickness of the modern world is the loss of confidence in any abiding significance of the transitory goods of life. For evidence we may cite the contemporary existentialist philosophy in which nothing matters but the moment of experience. Its consequence is the hell depicted in Sartre's *No Exit*. The possibility that our civilization and perhaps even the human race itself might be destroyed in atomic warfare has but given new intensity to the problem which has always haunted man the creature.[3]

If hopelessness breeds paralysis of will, hope releases human energies. The causes which enlist men always give some assurance that what is to be sacrificed for will bear fruitful consequences in some new order. The dynamic of fascism, communism, and democracy is in each case related to a faith in which each individual can see his life linked with a significant future. Hitler promised the thousand year Reich, the Marxists believe in the inevitability of the classless society, Democrats proclaim the century of the common man.

The Christian interpretation of man's pilgrimage in time cannot be put into a simple parallelism with these political philosophies. Christianity does not ignore the vision of a redeemed political order but it sets all political hopes in a perspective which relates each person and each historical fact to the ultimate community of all life with God. A Christian view of time and history which preserves the truth and rejects the illusion in man's vision of history can organize and release human energies today as it did in the days of St. Augustine, and as it did in the bright days of the nineteenth century when the prospect of a reborn society on earth seemed to light the way.

If a new vision of man's destiny is to come it will have to be founded on something different from the liberal theory of progress, and also something different from the complete rejection of that idea in contemporary theology. In this chapter I shall state the reasons for saying that the liberal doctrine will not do, and then try to save out of the liberal perspective the valid concept which it possessed. We can then examine the views of history of those who reject entirely the concept of the progress of man toward the Kingdom of God. Finally, we shall state the key concept by which a Christian conception of history can maintain fidelity to the facts and yield a more sobered but still hopeful view of the long pilgrimage of man.

II

The notion of a cumulative achievement of good in history which brings about in the world a more complete embodiment of the divine order was an integral part of the liberal Christian theology. What is often overlooked in the reaction against this doctrine is that the liberals formulated it in more than one way. Actually the conception of a cumulative achievement in our moral and religious experience is not easy to discard. Reinhold Niebuhr, for example, carefully insists that there are cumulative achievements on the plane of history.[4] Paul Tillich, in his discussion of the idea of progress, distinguishes several spheres to which the idea may be related: the first is that of technical progress, the second, that of political unification, and the third, "the gradual humanization of human relationships." In these, he agrees, progress has actually taken place. But there are two areas where the idea of progress does not apply: There is no progress with respect to the creative works of culture or with respect to the morality of mankind. The first is impossible because creativity is a matter of grace, not of growth; the second is impossible because morality is a matter of free decision, and consequently not a matter of delivery and tradition.[5]

These distinctions are clarifying, yet if they are held without qualification they deny the truth that the liberal theology was groping for, even though it never set it free from an untenable doctrine of the progressive elimination of evil from human life. This judgment may be sustained by examining briefly some of the formulas by which liberals sought to interpret the progress of the Kingdom of God in history.

Professor Case's *The Christian Philosophy of History* shows clearly the difficulties of interpreting history as the simple triumph of good men over evil men. His pattern is the liberal one:

> God is working within history where he has willed that men should learn to be the efficient instruments of the divine energy. Upon their shoulders has been placed the responsibility for learning and pursuing God's designs for bringing his Kingdom to realization on earth.[6]

History resolves itself into a conflict of good men with bad men. Badness is the result of a beastly strain "inherited perhaps from a Neanderthal man."[7] Case does not quite say the complete eradication of evil will ever be accomplished but still "the accumulations of the years mount ever upward toward the goal of the good man's desire."[8]

The moralism which makes possible such a neat separation between good and evil men, and which implies subtly that we who make the distinction are to be counted among the good cannot be refuted by argument. But once this simple removal of our own consciences from the sphere of judgment has been shaken, once we see the conflict between good and evil in its true depth in every human heart, a deeper view of history must be found if we are to have a hope based on solid foundations. Even on Case's terms the question of the meaning of the whole process remains unsolved. What is the meaning of the life of an individual with all its suffering and frustration if it be but a stage on the way to some future consummation in an infinitely removed time? In what sense is life fulfilled now? The problem is especially acute when we recognize as Case himself does that "a closer scrutiny of the historical process shows that disasters overtake equally the righteous with the wicked."[9] Christian liberalism must rewrite its philosophy of history with this fact given its full value. If we make a less simple distinction between the righteous and the wicked, and treat the problem of fulfillment in relation to the mystery of temporal flux and its relation to the abiding realities, then the Christian philosophy of history will stand

upon the belief in a redemptive activity of God which wins its
strange victory in spite of the continuing tragic character of the
course of events.

The interpretation of cosmic progress which Whitehead offers in
his *Adventures of Ideas* is not subject to quite the same criticism. He
takes the fundamental conflict to be that between force and persuasion.

The history of ideas is a history of mistakes. But through all mistakes it
is also the history of the gradual purification of conduct. When there is
progress in the development of favorable order, we find conduct protected
from relapse into brutalization by the increasing agency of ideas con-
sciously entertained. In this way Plato is justified in his saying, "The
creation of the world—that is to say, the world of civilized order—is the
victory of persuasion over force."[10]

The progress of mankind can be measured by this yardstick. Note
Whitehead's insistence that conduct is "protected from relapse."
The fact of progress was symbolized for Whitehead in the year he
wrote, 1931, by the achievement of a peaceful settlement between
Gandhi and the Viceroy of India.[11]

Waiving for the moment the far from settled question of the extent that Gandhi's techniques of nonviolence were adapted to the
particular social and cultural situation in which he found himself,
we still must ask whether we can really see the vindication of hope
for the higher values in a cumulative and secure achievement of
orders of persuasion over brute force. Certainly the experience of
the twentieth century confirms the fear that cultures of high moral
sensitivity may yet relapse into incredible cruelty. Whitehead's doctrine does not seem to square with his own view that there is an
element of conflict and exploitation in the very structure of life.
"Life is robbery."[12] Nor does his view square with the contem-
plation of the tragic element in the vision of God with which his
Process and Reality closes.[13]

The case may be put this way. If new configurations of power are always to be expected in the ongoing march of creativity, what reason have we to believe that the persuasive elements in life will not forever have to maintain a precarious existence amidst the formidable march of more ruthless powers? We must not discount the significance or worth of the "tendernesses" of life.[14] We may well account them more valuable just because they are precious amidst staggering forces. Yet the evidence seems slim indeed that the history of the cosmos exhibits a universal and progressive taming of the elemental forces. Whitehead himself has called for the cleansing of dogma by the recourse to critical analysis of the evidence. His view of history has a romantic overtone which goes beyond the facts.

A similar difficulty is presented by John Macmurray's attempt to combine a Christian-Augustinian doctrine of God's sovereignty with a Marxist interpretation of the structure of historical development as leading inevitably toward the fulfillment of the good society. Macmurray gives content to the doctrine that man is created in the image of God by saying this means we are created for freedom and for equality. The community defined by these two concepts is what our human nature really craves, and what it must have if it is not to be in conflict with itself both within the individual and within society. Therefore, any social structure which separates men into classes produces overt conflict between classes. Out of these conflicts the more adequate order of freedom and equality must certainly emerge, for it represents the embodiment of the real structure of historical forces which possess ultimately irresistible power. In his *Clue to History* in 1939 Macmurray wrote:

It is the inevitable destiny of fascism to create what it intends to prevent —the socialist commonwealth of the world. The fundamental law of human nature cannot be broken. "He that saveth his life shall lose it." The will to power is self-frustrating. It is the meek who will inherit the earth.[15]

Macmurray himself seems to allow some sort of qualification of this determinism. He says that "unless progress can be stopped altogether" his prediction stands.[16] But if stopping progress is a real possibility then the view that history is simply the carrying out of the intention of God must be restated.

All the paradoxes and difficulties of determinist views of history appear in Macmurray's treatment of freedom. The achievement of the divine intention is inevitable; yet men are called upon to "make the effort" on which depends the future of Western civilization.[17] If men must be rallied to "make an effort" in our historical period, an effort which they may fail to make, why may it not be so in every historical period? Macmurray's interpretation of the course of history has the advantage which comes from a realistic acceptance of the fact of conflict and tragedy in history. Yet like its Marxist counterpart his view is utopian in outcome, and falls into the error of all utopianism, that of endowing some particular historical movement or group with a moral significance and purity which it does not rightfully possess. So Macmurray says:

> Soviet Russia is the nearest approach to the realization of the Christian intention that the world has yet seen, for the intention of a universal community based on equality and freedom, overriding differences of nationality, race, sex, and "religion," is its explicit and conscious purpose.[18]

One does not have to indulge in hysterical anticommunist sentiment to detect the exaggeration and illusion in this statement.

Let us summarize the three difficulties which all theories of historical progress toward the Kingdom of God inherently involve, and at the same time try to extract from the liberal doctrine the element of truth which it certainly embodies.

There is, first, that aspect of the passage of time which makes it a threat to the enduring worth of all the particular carriers of value which we know. "Time is perpetual perishing," says Whitehead following Locke. If the worth of life is to be secured, we must find some sense in which, again in Whitehead's words, the occasions of experience "live forever more."[19] No matter how we try to tell ourselves that each moment has its value regardless of its endurance, we cannot be indifferent to the fact that the running stream of time bears away all that we cherish. Unless religious faith faces the possibility that the human race on this earth is not a permanent fixture in the scheme of things, its hope must be forever based on concealment. The humanist Max Otto closes his survey of the human enterprise with words of ringing promise:

> Oh, walk together children,
> Don't you get weary,
> There's a great Camp Meeting in the Promised Land.[20]

It is noteworthy that the humanist turns to the language of the religious tradition to express this conclusion. But on what basis does he hold out such a promise? We do not know what may be the fate of humanity in the course of cosmic history. The question of what may happen to life some billions of years from now is perhaps too remote to have any consequence in our thinking, except as it reminds us of the precarious situation of all life. Professor Gamow, the physicist, says our scientific knowledge gives us reason to expect that within some billions of years life will have been ended by the increasingly intense heat of the sun unless technical development may have made it possible to transport the race to some cooler portion of the universe.[21] This speculation takes on grim present significance when we contemplate the possibility that humanity now may have in biological and atomic weapons the means to make earth uninhabitable.

Religious hope clings to something deeper than the continuing chance that something will turn up to keep life going. It also rests on something deeper than speculation about an infinitely prolonged life in the form of what is often meant by immortality of the soul. It depends upon the insight that the value of life is conserved by an enduring and healing fact, the fact of God. How this truth is to be expressed is indeed a perplexing problem.

Though the liberal doctrines of progress did not squarely face the fact that "nature intends to kill man," there was an element in the liberal view of the meaning of the temporal character of life which is valid. It is that the risk and adventure in the process of life is itself a meaning and a value. As Winfred E. Garrison has suggested, "being on the way" in some sense forms part of the goal of life.[22]

The passage of time is not wholly a sentence of death upon value; it is also the form of creative effort and moral achievement. Life in time is life in decision. Without decision there can be nothing of the spiritual stature which gives to our existence its real worth. If our life is merely an imitation of eternity then it is but a game, and of no consequence. Involvement in process is itself an enduring value. We cannot imagine any good without it. Certainly it is an error to suppose that process and progress are synonymous. But it is a valid insight to see process as integral to the spiritual character of our existence. It is significant that there are an increasing number of those who believe that God's life itself must be conceived as having an element of adventure and movement into an open future, else we cannot conceive that He enters sympathetically into our human experience.[23]

The second problem in the theory of progress is involved in the fact of freedom. Reinhold Niebuhr points out the dilemma of liberal thought which has insisted on the freedom of man to guide his own life, and yet which has tried to imagine that this freedom will be progressively used only for the good. But moral freedom is freedom to rebel against the moral claim, and freedom of the spirit is freedom to rebel against God. The conclusion is inescapable that so long as man is free the risks of freedom must be admitted with all the possibilities of its misuse.

Even the most individualistic liberalism we may still say clung to an important insight in its conception of the meaning of freedom. The use of freedom is the participation of one life in the lives of others. Freedom means the opportunity to decide how one's life shall enter into the continuum of conditions and consequences. We have no freedom to decide whether we shall "give our lives away" in the continuing social process. We are always giving them away either constructively or destructively. The meaning of life is participation in an ongoing flow of activities in which the good of all participants is either served or blocked.'

In the philosophic tradition it is the idealists rather than the naturalists who have made the fullest place for this insight into the essentially social character of human existence, though contemporary naturalism as in Mead, Dewey, and Wieman has achieved a similar perspective. There is now emerging a reconciliation of the emphasis on individual freedom and the fact of the involvement of every creature in social structures. My life is not my own. It is the result of the creative activity of God in a stream of conditions and events far beyond the range of my knowledge. My conscious life is but a faint light shining out of a background of powers, processes, events, and memories. In every moment of life, I give my being back into the stream. I am actually in large measure what others can take me to be. My own self is completed only as others are affected by my being. I am passive to the social process in every moment and yet an active creator of it. Within this taking and giving the marvelous fact of free, responsible reflection and decision appears. Now this self which decides freely is not apart from the social process, but rather embedded in it. Yet in some degree it can in its own integrity freely choose what it shall accept and reject from the whole, and thus it chooses in part the way in which it shall enter into the experience of others. What I decide becomes a datum for others and the consequences of my decision a part of their objective world.

In some such fashion we can do justice to the elements of determination and freedom in our experience. Only individuals have minds, but each mind is what it is in large part because of what it has received from the group. Hence the group is something more than a collection of individuals' minds; the group is a process in which individual minds are woven together in a dynamic pattern which tends to impose itself on each one.

The liberal gain in the interpretation of freedom can still be held. Freedom means the possibility to allow ourselves to be determined by that which is deepest in the process of life; and to relate our own lives to the ongoing whole in decisions made out of faith, hope, and love. Freedom is the opportunity to qualify the structure of life for ourselves and for others. It is the possibility of maintaining integrity by serving first the good of God and all other things second. To affirm this possibility is not to claim that in human experience it is ever perfectly actualized. But it is to recognize that our human decisions are made possible by our appropriation of the meanings, memories, hopes, and possibilities which become available to us in the history in which we live.

The judgment that there can be no progress in the moral realm is not defensible. Unless there be some cumulative and progressive development of the community of freedom, equality, and love among men it is impossible to give any adequate account of our common experience of sharing in the spirit and insight which comes to us from others. It is this sharing which makes our own moral decision possible. We are members one of another, even in moral experience. Every parent's concern for the kind of environment in which his child grows up is testimony to this fact, even though we know that we can never *guarantee* the quality of life which will emerge in any free person.

The final problem for the progressive view is that of the actual fact of the persistence of evil in all the structures of human history. There are varieties of Christian experience with the evil in the self. For some the break with sin appears to be possible; for others, there is the continuing experience, "that which I would I do not, and that which I would not that I do." But in either case we cannot say that any life is beyond the power of temptation and sin. We know of no social order which does not show exploitation and injustice, none in which tragic choices do not have to be made. There is a rent in existence, and its name is evil. All that it means we cannot know.

The Christian theologian, John Bennett, has powerfully stated this truth in his *Christian Realism*.[24]

While the belief in the cumulative processes of life permits us no superficial optimism, it does require the acknowledgment that the final meaning of evil cannot be known until all things are done. There is, we do know, a redemptive work of God through which past evil, while it remains evil, can enter into the creation of present good by qualifying our moral sensitivity, and deepening our valuation of life. There can be moral maturing through tragic experience both for individuals and for whole peoples. Out of the suffering of the Hebrew people has come the moral power of the prophets and the spiritual reality of reconciliation between man and God.

Liberal theology made its contribution to theology through its affirmation of process as the most fundamental category of being. The Christian interpretation of the meaning of history becomes transformed when this conception is allowed to replace the metaphysics of static being. It should be possible to restate the Christian hope for God's work with man in history from this new perspective without falling into the errors of those who allowed process to become too simply identified with progress.[25] But before we come to our constructive statement, it is necessary to examine the alternative treatment of this problem in neo-orthodox thought today.

III

An alternative to the interpretation of history as process is offered today in those Christian theologies which have been influenced by existential philosophy which has its primary source in Kierkegaard. It is argued that process metaphysics takes the measured or clock time of physics and identifies it with the time which is relevant to human decisions and to freedom. This identification is said to be untenable. The time form of freedom is another structure, related in some way to clock time, but never to be identified with the

sequential order of natural processes. Nicolas Berdyaev who affirms
the existential point of view summarizes the position: "There are
three times: cosmic time, historical time; and existential time."
Cosmic time is symbolized by the circle, it is calendar or clock time.
Historical time is that of memory and prospect. It is always broken.
The moments pass away and are not fulfilled. Its symbol is the line.
Berdyaev says:

> Existential time must not be thought of in complete isolation from
> cosmic and historical time, it is a break-through of one time into the
> other. . . . Existential time may be best symbolized not by the circle or by
> the line but by the point. . . . This is inward time . . . not objectivized. It
> is the time of the world of subjectivity, not objectivity. . . . Every state of
> ecstasy leads out from the computation of objectivized mathematical time
> and leads into existential qualitative infinity.[26]

These distinctions appear in various forms in Kierkegaard, Cull-
man, Minear, Niebuhr, and Tillich, and in each case they are used
for the interpretation of the Biblical world view. And in each case
the history of salvation is interpreted as belonging to a superhistory
which transcends the cosmic process.

Let us try to formulate as accurately as possible what is being
affirmed in this existential theory. When man confronts the question of the meaning of his life he finds that the question can only
be answered if he sees that he is related to a transcendent reality,
a God whose being is of a different order from that of all creatures
and processes in our experience, who is the "unconditioned" ground
of all being, to use Tillich's phrase. Since the meaning of life lies
in man's relation to God so conceived, the dimension of our being
with which religion is concerned involves something other than any
experienced process immanent in existence. The meaning of life
cannot be measured in relation to a structure of value discoverable
in our existence. When we speak therefore of Creation, of God's
purposes, of the times in which God reveals Himself, and when
we speak of the end of all things, the coming of the Kingdom,

we use temporal terms but we are not speaking of events to which a date can be assigned. To be sure in the case of the revelation in Jesus Christ, to take the most important example, the time of salvation is intimately connected with an actual historical period and date. But we are speaking of a realm of meaning which is not bound by the categories of historical experience. We can apprehend the meaning of what we say only in the moment and in the act of decision or, as Berdyaev says, in ecstasy. The ultimate reality upon which our hope depends is therefore the eternal truth and power of God, breaking into the flow of historical events, qualifying it, transforming it, yet always to be understood as giving meaning to life through its relation to that which is beyond the time form of the world process.

So far at least I understand Kierkegaard and his followers. This standpoint represents the sharpest possible challenge to the liberal theology with its affirmation that the natural processes are the locus of God's redemptive work; and that the meaning of life is organically involved in the emergence of orders of value in history.

This problem is so fundamental to the whole question of the nature of Christian hope and the existential analysis is so widely influential that I propose to examine Kierkegaard's formulation more closely and to offer a criticism of it.

Sören Kierkegaard is the most important source and the magnificent genius of existential philosophy. If a reconstruction in theology which is neither liberal nor neo-orthodox is to emerge it will have to define itself against Kierkegaard even as Kierkegaard defined himself against Hegel. And it will, I believe, learn much from Kierkegaard as he learned much from the great idealist.

Hegel's philosophy is a thoroughgoing and grandiloquent attempt to conceive the whole of world history as a process exhibiting a rational structure. It is the spirit coming to self-consciousness, God realizing Himself in human society. That Hegel badly overstated and overworked his thesis is universally recognized. He did have a profound sense of the tragic and the ironic in human affairs. He was not a naïve optimist; but he did not avoid the idolatry of identifying the absolute will of God with the Prussian state in which he happened to live and work.[27]

Kierkegaard's work is a sustained and passionate protest against the Hegelian system, and against what Hegel made out of human history, and out of Christianity. Where Hegel saw continuity and rational pattern, Kierkegaard saw discontinuity and paradox. Hegel and his followers felt intellectually secure in the logical structure which underlay the System. Kierkegaard attacked this complacency with savage irony and invective. When Hegelianized theology became the means of fortifying the complacencies of the established Christian Church, Kierkegaard literally poured out his life in a struggle to expose what to him was a betrayal of the Christ who suffered and died that men might repent.

For Kierkegaard the human soul is poised on the knife edge of lostness. He tried to break through Hegelian objectivity to the inwardness and suffering of personal existence. No Christian before him, and perhaps none since, has so profoundly expressed the desperation of the soul's search for a rock of faith which will hold firm in the midst of the complete insecurity of human existence. These things Kierkegaard felt, and he said them with a penetration of the human heart and a consummate artistry rarely equaled in either philosophical or theological writing. I do not see how one can read him and remain the same person. We turn eagerly to learn the secret of that leap of faith which gains assurance of God and through which a man becomes a disciple of the Christ who is contemporary with every age.[28]

Just here the perplexities begin. Kierkegaard describes this movement toward God, or this being met by God, in terms which remove it from any recognizable human experience. He insists that his philosophy makes a place for real becoming where Hegel's "becoming" is all shadow play.[29] Becoming is defined by Kierkegaard as "a change in actuality brought about by freedom."[30] But this becoming takes place in the moment of existential time. It is no process in the time sequence of human events. "If a decision in time is postulated then . . . the learner is in error, which is precisely what makes a beginning in the moment necessary."[31] The knife of existential analysis cuts cleanly between the past and present in describing the new birth. "In the *Moment* man also becomes conscious of the new birth, for his antecedent state was one of non-being."[32]

What is this movement which takes place outside of time; which is a leap from non-Being to Being without even so much as the Hegelian dialectical logic to connect the two stages? The closest Kierkegaard comes to giving a philosophical answer is his notion of repetition. The Socratic "recollection" will not do, for that is recall of something temporally past. There must be a movement toward eternity which is movement toward realization but not in a temporal sense. This he calls repetition. This concept never received very clear definition from Kierkegaard but we are perhaps not far wrong if we say that repetition is man's free enactment of his relationship to eternity. For example, Kierkegaard is "repeating" Abraham's sacrifice of Isaac in his renunciation of his fiancée. In any case this conception cannot be made intelligible. Kierkegaard himself says that this category is the "interest upon which metaphysics founders."[33] The whole continuum of conditions and consequences in time is set aside. For the religious movement it does not exist.

Four unhappy consequences flow from Kierkegaard's doctrine of time. They have not been escaped in the neo-orthodox movement which he had greatly influenced, though some of his exaggerations have been sharply qualified. We should consider in our time of theological ferment what price must be paid for the existential doctrine that ultimate meaning belongs only to the Moment, that is, to a time which is other than the time of the world-historical process. It is, I suggest, too high a price, both in the loss of rational coher-

ence, and in loss of the relevance of religious faith to human
problems.

The first consequence is Kierkegaard's extreme individualism.
He declared his category was "the solitary individual" and desired
these words inscribed on his tomb.[34] It is, to be sure, something of
a relief in the midst of today's sentimentalities about "fellowship"
to hear Kierkegaard affirm that fellowship is a lower category than
the individual.[35] But he overshot his mark. He practically ignored
the significance of life in the social process, and in the religious
community. This was not accidental. Our common-sense view of
time regards it as the form of social process. It is the order which
links past with future in the continuum of influences and consequences. But Kierkegaard's "Moment" is apart from all this. In the
crisis of decision a man may think of himself as freed from all
external relations. So Kierkegaard apparently thinks. But this is an
illusion. It is a distortion of the facts to say that "the disciple who
is born anew owes nothing to any man but everything to his Divine
Teacher."[36] We are not solitary individuals, even in the moment
of decision. What happens in the moment of choice owes much to
our inheritance from the communities in which our lives are lived.
Kierkegaard's own individualism is partly explicable in relation to
his experience of discovering that he was not "like the others."[37]

The issue here joined with existential philosophy involves much
more than philosophical technicalities. It is a matter of life and
death to our civilization that we recover what it means to possess
freedom in community. Real freedom belongs not to the isolated
individual, but to the person who can maintain his individuality
and integrity even as he accepts his interdependence with other life.
If theology is to illuminate the life of the human spirit it must
interpret both the fact of man's capacity to judge society from a
point of view which transcends all achieved cultural values, and
also the fact of that social solidarity which in the religious com-

munity makes the prophetic critic possible. Isaiah and Jeremiah spoke for their people Israel even as they spoke against them.

The second consequence is that the time-form of religious decision is divorced from the time-form of political and social effort. Kierkegaard confesses he knows and cares nothing about politics. Amusingly he says his acquaintances charge him with being politically "a nincompoop who bows seven times before everything that has a royal commission." It is not altogether a satisfactory answer that he is serving the kingdom which "would not at any price be a kingdom of this world."[38] The question of responsible decision in the political order remains. To say that "there exists only one sickness, sin,"[39] and to pour scorn on all political movements produces a simplification of human problems, and in some instances prophetic judgment; but it also leaves the manipulation of social and political institutions which do make and break lives of people to whatever shrewd and ruthless schemers may get social power.

A third consequence follows inevitably. Kierkegaard denies all meaning to moral progress in history. The sharpness of his analysis enables us to recognize the real problem but it also discloses the inadequacy of his answer. He holds that all ages and times stand under the same judgment of God. "Every generation has to begin all over again with Christ."[40] He contrasts the idea of the Church Militant in which the Christian stands in opposition to his culture, with the idea of the Church Triumphant (on earth), in which the Christian is honored and rewarded for being a Christian. The first he believes is Christianity, the second hypocrisy.[41] Therefore, "if the contemporary generation of believers found no time to triumph, neither will any later generation, for the task is always the same and faith is always militant."[42]

Now in one sense the task always is the same. It is to transform men who try to live life apart from God into men who begin to trust God. No human progress can change the fundamental necessity of that movement in every age and time. But it does not follow that all societies and cultures offer equally adequate contexts for making the transformation possible for more and more persons. The Church grows in a time of persecution. But we do not therefore work for the creation of a society so inhuman and unjust that any who seek justice and love will be cast into prison, tortured and killed. Let us substitute our own paradox for Kierkegaard's. The task of serving the Kingdom of God will always be the same. But that task includes the everlasting effort to bring decency and justice into human society. While that aspect of the task is never finished, it is not without its real successes, or its hope for greater ones.

A final consequence of Kierkegaard's view is that it becomes inconceivable how God can share in the actual processes of human experience. "The eternal . . . has absolutely no history."[43] Therefore, we can make nothing of the conception of God as patient and suffering worker. The meaning of our existence as unfinished creatures in a life which has its times of planting and its times of reaping becomes an insoluble riddle. I do not say Kierkegaard accepts this conclusion in all respects. But it is inherent in his view of time.

Many of the extreme consequences of Kierkegaard's position are avoided by those contemporary theologians who have gone through existentialism to the reconstruction of Biblical theology, and who have sought to discover, usually with Kierkegaard's help, the "unique time-consciousness" of the Bible.[44]

This assertion that there is a distinctive time-consciousness in the Biblical world view is made by Professor Paul Minear. His studies in Biblical theology show that there is in the Bible the basis for a corrective of the exaggerated individualism of Kierkegaard. The Bible grows out of historical experience and its world view involves a profound sense of the meaning of the life of peoples, their hopes and expectancies, their time of crisis, and their ultimate destiny. But Professor Minear's interpretation of the Biblical outlook falls short just at the point where he insists on reading the Bible through the eyes of Kierkegaard.

Minear points out that the Bible speaks of time in two senses, which are usually designated by two different words, *chronos* and *kairos*.[45] *Chronos* refers to calendar time, *kairos* to historical and eschatological time. The *"kairos"* is the "crucial stage in destiny." It is the time of decision which involves man's ultimate destiny.

It is characteristic of the tendency of neo-orthodox thought, even when it returns to the Biblical conception of time, to make the distinction between *kairos* and *chronos* too sharp. The distinction is made in such a way that *chronos*, the day-by-day time which is the form of our human existence, is either treated as irrelevant to the issues of man's salvation, or else it is regarded as the sphere of death and frustration from which we must be saved. Minear seems to be imposing a metaphysical distinction on the Bible when he says that the coming of Christ means that "the tyranny of *chronos* has been broken once and for all. It stands under the all-encompassing negation of God's judgment. Its boundary has been set by the manifestation of a 'wholly-other order of reality.' "[46] But why, we ask, must *chronos* be negated? Is it wholly evil in God's sight or man's experience that there should be times and seasons? Does the Bible really separate a calendar time which is the sphere of tragic frustration from a time which is wholly different? It appears rather that the Bible views the history of the Hebrew people, the life of Jesus, and the life of the Church as sharing in one continuous working of God in which every aspect of human life and its natural environment has its necessary and fruitful role to play. There are difficulties indeed with the Biblical eschatology; but some of them arise precisely from the fact that the Biblical world view did not contemplate a distinction between two orders of time. The world, it is said, was created in six days. The end of the world is an event expected before those now living pass away. When the Apostle Paul says, "It is far on in the night the day is almost here," and when

John says, "It doth not *yet* appear what we shall be,"[47] they transcend the distinction between *chronos* and *kairos*. Both are within the sphere of God's redemptive purpose. It is difficult to see how, if God's relationship to the world is "wholly other" than the relation of creative spirit to its actual working in time (chronos), we can avoid discounting the Christian significance of creative effort, patient workmanship, and that careful assessment of conditions and consequences which make up so large a part of the wisdom of life.

Such an outcome which is both un-Biblical and irrational can be avoided by a restatement of the meaning of time. The concrete reality of life is the community of created beings in their individuality and their togetherness. This community moves in a continuous stream from the past into the future. God is the supreme and uncreated member of this community. We are therefore members of Him and of one another. The time structure of this interweaving of processes is duration. This is time as the order characterizing the flow of process.

Chronos, then and *kairos* are abstractions. They are structures which our minds can distinguish in the concrete reality for the purpose of speaking intelligibly about it. *Kairos* abstracts the elements of meaning, valuation, purpose, and expectation. Both terms designate something less than the full meaning of duration which escapes adequate interpretation. Yet on this view we can say that God enters into the experience of man. Both *chronos* and *kairos* have meaning for God. Professor Hartshorne's statement of the relation of God to time saves what is intellectually and religiously meaningful in the Biblical conception.

God is the cosmic "adventure" (Whitehead) integrating all real adventures as they occur, without ever failing in readiness to realize new states out of the divine potency, which is indeed "beyond number" and definite form, yet is of value only because number and form come out of it.[48]

It follows that one dimension of the meaning of the Christian life is our share in world-building. It means we accept the process of becoming with all the tasks of politics, education, and reconstruction, as the area where some of God's work gets done. We may thus preserve a unity in life. Such unity is lost if we say that the time in which we prepare today for tomorrow is of another and lesser order from the time in which we encounter God.

IV

When we attempt to do justice to all aspects of the problem of the nature of progress in human history we discover we must try to hold two truths together. The first is that our life is a process. Every moment of experience enters into and qualifies the continuous stream of life in and through which God works. The second truth is that there is a cleft which runs through the whole of our existence. Possibilities remain unrealized. There is real evil, and real loss. We live on the boundary line between the actual and the potential good. We cannot see the whole, or the end. Life resembles a poem the last line of which has not been written. Yet the meaning of the whole depends upon it. We know what it is to participate in God's cumulative victory over the chaos of existence. Yet the victory is not yet won. We know that God works creatively and redemptively to overcome all that estranges us from Him. Yet we continually cry out, How long, O Lord, how long?

It is absurd to think that a simple formula can interpret the mystery of man's pilgrimage. But the discussion so far suggests the possibility that a new Christian perspective on history may be emerging which will hold together the truth in the liberal doctrine of progress and the truth in the neo-orthodox affirmation of the judgment of God upon all existing things. We have now reached the point in our argument where the proposed synthesis can be formulated. Every interpretation of the meaning of history has its guiding image. We need a key concept with which to draw together the many strands of truth about one history. There is such a concept in the New Testament. Both liberalism and neo-orthodoxy have done it less than justice. It is the concept of our present history as proceeding under the reign of Christ. But the Christ who reigns in our history is embattled with his enemies. The Biblical source of this image is Paul's word in the eschatological passage of I Corinthians 15. "He must reign till he hath put all his enemies under his feet. The last enemy that shall be destroyed is death."[49] He has already despoiled the principalities and powers in the victory of the cross yet he remains the embattled Christ, contending with all things which stand in the way of God's fulfillment of His redemptive work.[50] Professor John Knox summarizes the Biblical view of our human situation after Christ has entered our history in the life and death of Jesus:

> Sin is doomed and its power is weakened, but it has not been actually destroyed: salvation has already been bestowed in Christ, but the fulfillment of that salvation awaits Christ's return in glorious power to bring to completion his victory over sin and death and to inaugurate fully and finally the Kingdom of God.[51]

Biblical concepts should not be strait jackets for the mind, but wings for it. They guard in metaphorical terms the fundamental insights which have come through God's revelation to the prophets, and through the impact of Jesus upon the world. We can use the conception of the embattled reign of Christ as a guide to a reformulation of the Christian view of history. In the end this symbolic expression can have just so much meaning for us as we can give it through specifying that in our experience which bears it out. It is a Christian symbol which can form the key to a more realistic theology than that which conceived of "building the Kingdom of God in history." It is a symbol which can be the basis for understanding between the American social gospel and the Continental insistence that God's Kingdom cannot be identified with human schemes. It can be the basis for a realistic expression of the Christian hope. We know that we live as sinners in social structures and spiritual climates which corrupt our souls, and which plunge us toward horrible catastrophe. But we know also that these powers have not the last word. They can be broken. They have been exposed through the revelation culminating in Jesus Christ. We could not even recognize them for what they are if we were not living in the beginning of a new order where love dwells.

Let us be specific about what it means to say we live in that history which is determined by the reign of Christ in conflict with his enemies.

We mean, first, that through what God has accomplished in the events which came to their climax in the life of Jesus our human existence has been given a new structure. Creative and redemptive power has been released in it which was not wholly released before. We see a meaning in life which was not so fully discerned before. There is a new community in history. Members of that community begin to live on the basis of what has taken hold of them through the life of Jesus.

The reign of Christ, then, is that period in human history which is interpreted by Christians through what God has done in the life of Jesus to disclose the ultimate meaning of our existence. That meaning is life in the community of love. It is the *logos* of our being. The *logos* is God Himself known to us under the form of the Christ-figure.[52] There is an endless variety of ways in which men respond to this disclosure of God. They may ignore it, reject it, despise the view of life to which it gave rise. Or they may begin to live life in response to the truth and power there given. What is given to us through God's revelation includes the ethic of outgoing and forgiving love. It includes the knowledge of our radical dependence upon God's grace which goes out to those who are not worthy of it. It includes the depth and mystery of the suffering of God known to us through the suffering of Jesus upon the cross. And it includes the new life of the Christian as the enactment of the way

of love in a community of those who live in this faith. It is possible
to speak of such a life only because we acknowledge that it depends
wholly upon our participation in the working of God which is
infinitely deeper than anything we can define or control. Only as
Christ reigns can we serve one another in love.

While we affirm the release of the power of God as the meaning
of the reign of Christ it must be understood that that power is no
arbitrary and ruthless force. Certainly it is true that God does exercise coercive power. We cannot escape that fact when we look
at the way in which the structures of life coerce us, smash our plans,
seize us in the grip of their inevitabilities. God is not identical with
those structures but His wrath is in them as they are related to the
ultimate structure of value which is His own being. But God also
works persuasively; and His supreme resource is not coercive force,
but the compelling power of His revelation in the Suffering Servant
of all. The Christ who reigns asserts God's power as truly in the
washing of the feet of the disciples as in the condemnation of the
Pharisees. He transforms the world as he dies upon the cross, even
as he transforms it in expelling the money-changers from the
temple. We should not absolutize any one event in the life of Jesus
as disclosing the way in which God's love must work. The ethical
implications of this position we shall shortly examine. But here it
is necessary to point out that when we speak of the reigning Christ
we do not mean the monarchical concept of an arbitrary exercise
of power. Christ reigns supremely because he reigns from his cross.[53]

This conception of the reign of Christ includes the universality
of his meaning for human existence. Here is the bridge between
the social gospel and the neo-orthodox theology. There are not two
kingdoms, one an inner kingdom of Christ related only to believers,
and another a kingdom of this world which God has left to other
powers, and upon which His love makes no immediate demands.
That conception was destroyed long ago by the social gospel with
its affirmation of the Christian concern with the structure of human

society. It is also being vigorously criticized by the continental theologians today. Karl Barth himself perhaps even fell into an exaggerated identification of a political cause with the cause of Christ in some of his writings during the war.[54] In any case the Christian affirmation is that the reign of Christ involves a demand for justice and freedom throughout the whole of life. Nothing less than the whole is the field of God's redemptive work.

In the second place, to live in the reign of Christ means to share in an actual and continual victory of good over evil. It is one thing to recognize that evil is never eradicated from the self or from society. But it does not follow that good never triumphs over evil. The fact is quite the contrary. There would be no world at all, if there were not a continual realization of good. Every achievement of good is in so far a victory over evil, either over the evil of chaos and meaninglessness, or the evil of actual obstructions to the growth of the real good. Christians ought always to take heart. It is not true that there are no historical gains making for a humanity which more nearly exemplifies the image of its creator. There is always something to be done in the service of God under the reign of Christ. While we have admitted we cannot from our human point of view guarantee the permanence of any created good we know; we do know that wherever conditions of slavery, ignorance, and established privilege have been broken there is a gain which man can surrender only at the cost of denying that which is deepest in himself.

Perhaps men will deny their own will for life in community. The reign of Christ is always an embattled reign. Our third assertion is that we know nothing of the working of God in the world except in relation to real opposition. Christ's reign is embattled in the human spirit, in the social structures, and in the Church which is his own body in the world. Protestant hope for the Church is not based upon any notion of its freedom from the corruptions of sin. It is based on the fact that in the Church among all human communities men can most directly appeal to the reigning Christ's judgment upon the community itself. The Church is not the Kingdom of God. It is the people who live by faith in the Christ who reigns against an opposition which exists even in those who have begun to serve him.

Christ is embattled with untruth. Our perspective applies in the realm of knowledge. "Now we see through a glass darkly."[55] We speak of the very essence of God's being. We know He is love. Yet we know that all human constructions in which we try to grasp this essence are inadequate.

The struggle with evil goes on "until Christ has put death under his feet." So far as we know human history will always be the scene of contending powers. But the conception of the reign of Christ contains a hope which looks beyond all the particular victories which God continues to win. This is our fourth assertion. Our hope is that the good which comes to be is not lost, but participates in the continuing life of God and thus shares in His ultimate victory. A consummation of history in which evil is finally purged and destroyed is beyond our power even to imagine. Hope does not depend upon it, though it may include it. But we do know that it means to share in a victory of God over the world in the sense that through faith in Him and His ultimate mercy we are reconciled to the conflict in which we stand. We believe that not only our present victories but even our failures can be transmuted into good. We believe that good is everlasting in God.

The question of the ultimate outcome of history involves the meaning of the Kingdom of God. We distinguish between the reign of Christ and the Kingdom of God. God's Kingdom is always present in history for it is His assertion of His love with power. It has come among us in Jesus Christ, whose reign is God's reign. But the Kingdom of God is also a symbol for the fulfillment of love in all things. That fulfillment is beyond the reign of Christ. It is an eschatological concept. It symbolizes an ultimate victory which we can know only as promise and share only in hope. Thus the concept of the reign of Christ enables us to make a clear distinction between what our human works achieve in history and the community of God's love in its perfect fulfillment. His Kingdom is always judgment upon our works, even while it is manifest in His power in our midst.

To live as a believer in the reign of Christ means to live within the battle not apart from it. It is no sham battle. But to believe that Christ reigns within the battle is to find peace. We know that God has His own strategy for bringing good out of evil. As believers we begin to live in a new history where love is accomplishing its perfect work, though this new history is never separate from the old. Again Paul's words express both the continuing struggle and the everlasting victory:

We are pressed on every side, yet not straitened; perplexed, yet not unto despair; pursued, yet not forsaken; smitten down, yet not destroyed; always bearing about in the body the dying of Jesus, that the life also of Jesus may be manifested in our body.[56]

With this interpretation of the Christian philosophy of human history we have reached the affirmation upon which our entire argument rests. Christian hope which gathers up all particular human hopes and yet is deeper than they is founded upon the fact of the present creative and redemptive working of God in human life. It remains to show what this implies for individual ethics, for social ethics, and for the progress toward spiritual maturity of the Christian. Our closing chapters are devoted to these three problems.

CHAPTER SIX

The Divine Call and Man's Response

IN THE conception of the meaning of history at which we have arrived we interpret our present life as having its course within and under the reign of Christ. God has revealed His love in Christ with decisive power and clarity. He has made it possible for us to believe in the victory of His love, and to see its beginnings. Yet the victory is not consummated.

It is necessary to consider the implications of this standpoint for Christian ethics. Our problem is to interpret the moral responsibility of the Christian in relation to the faith that God's grace is operative creatively and redemptively in life. If this can be done we shall have passed beyond the crisis of liberal Christianity; for the liberal view of the relation of Christian love to moral problems is in difficulty today precisely because the philosophy of history on which it is based does not sufficiently recognize the tragic obstacles which are set in the way of the life of love. Neo-orthodox theology is unable to give adequate ethical guidance, for, as we have seen, its philosophy of history commits an opposite error and puts the love of God outside of history. It is judgment upon us; but it does not transform the world.

I

Christian ethics must be practical as well as theoretical. The test of theory is its capacity to illuminate the concrete demands which God makes upon the use of our freedom in all the variety of human situations. But is not that problem solved for the Christian? The living God has spoken in the Ten Commandments, in His word given through the prophets, in the teaching and example of Jesus, in the Sermon on the Mount, in the two great commandments of love to God and to our neighbor. For Christian faith these are the disclosures of God's will. Yet to say this is really to state the problem rather than to solve it for three reasons.

The first is the obvious one that moral principles have to be interpreted. "Thou shalt not steal," can serve as an example. An advertiser slightly exaggerates the merits of a product in order to induce people to buy. Is that stealing? "Thou shalt not bear false witness." We withhold facts from someone for his own good. Is that lying? And what things are Caesar's?

The second difficulty is that the spirit of love is something more than principles and rules. This is the assertion of the freedom of the Gospel over against the bondage of the law. We serve a living God and we cannot believe that He has bound Himself to static requirements embedded in the past and its traditions. The spirit of love must work amidst the infinite variety of occasions and duties. Yet we know we cannot live without principles and rules.

Finally, there is the scandal of our moral situation. All of us, at all times, live in ways which serve evil as well as good, and which contradict the spirit of love. In proving this sweeping statement we need not single out some one example of our moral plight, such as our perplexity of conscience in the killing and destruction of war, and treat it as an isolated problem. It is not. It is an example, of especial difficulty to be sure, of the universal moral problem of man. How can we say we love and serve our neighbor when in many of our individual and social relations we exploit one another? Fritz Kreisler remarked not long ago that he never drinks a bottle of milk without realizing that he is taking it away from some child who needs it more than he does. As Lincoln Steffens wrote, "We

are in on the evils we abhor" in modern society.[1] When we try to
do our moral duty by working against these evils, we discover that
we rarely have a choice which does not involve compromise. Every
conscientious politician discovers what T. V. Smith has called the
deepest theoretical discrepancy in life, that between private conscience and public convenience.[2] We must support injustice and
profit from special privilege in order to possess power which may
make it possible for us to do some relative good. The Gospel in-
junction, "Be ye perfect," leaves us bewildered before what Woodbridge has called "earth's inappropriateness to perfection."[3]

In dwelling thus upon our ethical perplexities we must not
obscure the fact that our deepest problem is to find the strength
to do the right as we see it. The doing may help the seeing. If our
hearts were more nearly what they should be our minds would be
less confused. But there are real moral dilemmas. Growth in ethical
sensitivity often increases perplexity in the tragic choices of life.
Few of us today can read with anything but unbelieving astonish-
ment a statement by Phillips Brooks which breathes the spirit of
more serene days:

> The wonder of the life of Jesus is this . . . that there is not a single
> action that you are called upon to do of which you need be, of which you
> will be, in any serious doubt for ten minutes as to what Jesus Christ . . .
> would have you do under those circumstances and with the material upon
> which you are called to act.[4]

Dean Willard Sperry, whose theological orientation is perhaps not
very far removed from that of Phillips Brooks, speaks for us when
he says:

> All of us—manufacturers, industrialists, bankers, brokers, hand workers,
> professors, doctors, ministers—are involved together in the moral muddle
> and the moral tragedy of our time.[5]

It does not serve clarity on this point to indulge in the melan-
choly of moral despair. The very persistence of private conscience

in the face of public convenience supports the faith that moral values are not irrelevant. If we put to ourselves in honest self-examination this question, "When we try to think through to the end our actual moral responsibility before God, what do we see in our moral situation?" very likely the answer has a curious double aspect. On the one hand the difference between right and wrong stands out quite clearly. The distinction between an honest effort to secure justice and base connivance in injustice, the difference between loyalty and disloyalty to those we love, the difference between a decent and a vicious life—all of this becomes sharply outlined when we are honest. At the same time the absolute demands of the Gospel loom up more and more clearly as judgment upon us. The security and comfort which we enjoy are purchased at someone else's expense. The modern city, where more and more of us want to live, enjoys its munificence at the expense of the rural areas as Arthur E. Holt has forcibly brought home in *This Nation Under God.*[6] Those fortunate enough to live in suburbs or other desirable residential districts enjoy their space and light partly through the exploitation of the crowded and blighted areas. As a nation we waste enough food each day to keep thousands from starvation. But the waste goes on. The scramble for the more desirable niche in a crowded world continues, and we are in it.

Such is the scandal of our moral situation. We must find something deeper than a simple moralism in our approach to the moral problem itself. We must find how it is possible to hold to some ultimate integrity even when that integrity involves a radical humility about our own moral attainment. The religious life is always something more and deeper than "the good life."

What is demanded of Christian ethics in our time is to show how we can hold together the absolute claim of the God of love upon every life amidst the ambiguities of our moral situation. We must try again, as Christians have always tried, to find our way through the paradox of losing one's life to find it which appears finally in every ethical decision. We must put the answer not merely in generalities, but so as to guide the Christian service of God in the actual roles and decisions which are open to us. We must have an ethic for the president of General Corporation and the representatives of Local 42 as they face one another in a dispute over the closed shop. The policeman, the public executioner, the machine politician, the manufacturer of atomic bombs are not queer individuals with unique ethical problems. They are Everyman. Our debates over pacifism often obscure the fact that both the supporter of war who kills and the conscientious objector who risks allowing defenseless people to be killed both share the same fundamental moral dilemma in spite of their different ways of solving it. Christian ethics must make it clear how Christians who differ radically on specific ethical issues may yet find reconciliation and mutual support within the body of Christ.

There is, I suggest, a Christian answer to the moral problem, not in the form of a solution to every particular moral choice, but in the form of a deeper understanding of the moral life itself. This answer depends upon the theological insight that the God we serve is both Creator and Redeemer. The Christian answer lies in a conception which emerged in the Protestant Reformation, but which has yet to be appreciated in its full meaning: the conception of life as vocation.

II

We can throw the Protestant answer to the moral problem into clearer relief if we contrast it with the Roman Catholic solution.

For Roman Catholicism the final court of appeal in all moral questions is the Church, which interprets the revealed will of God. For Protestantism the final court of appeal is the conscience of the individual as he responds to the Word of God. There appears here clearly a certain initial advantage to the Catholic, for when he asks,

"How shall I know in a given case what I ought to do," he can always turn to the Church which claims to possess the infallible truth of God and which therefore claims to speak with final authority on every moral situation. The genius of Catholicism has been displayed in its achievement of uniting the moral teaching of the Bible with the rationalistic tradition of Aristotelian ethics, Stoicism, and the tradition of natural law, and in its continuing capacity to adjust and refine its moral tradition in the light of new situations. Elements of democratic ethics, such as doctrines of human rights and religious freedom, are gradually finding their way into Catholic thought.[7] Since the Church is a living organism it can respond to every new cultural situation while maintaining steadfastly its own absolute authority. The problem of the compromise of the Christian with the necessities of secular life is solved in Catholicism by the establishment within the Church of religious orders in which, through renunciation of "the world," the life of love can be realized and the moral merit thus achieved, shared with all the believers in the Church. Finally, the need for forgiveness of the Christian, whether he be a worldly sinner or a saint, is always met. The sacrifice of the mass makes it possible for the Christian to appropriate the supreme merit of Christ without whose atonement for our sin none of us could deserve anything but condemnation before the judgment of God.

Protestantism ought always to be conscious of the depth and scope of this Catholic solution of the problem of the Christian life. We may be alternately amused and amazed at a judgment like the following contained in a standard Catholic work on moral theology: "Catholic moral theology is based on the dogmatic teaching of the one true Church. Protestant ethics rests on arbitrary doctrinal assumptions. . . . Catholics acknowledge an infallible authority in questions of both dogma and morals, whereas Protestants possess no objective rule for either but are buffeted to and fro by the winds of subjectivism and error."[8] But we can admit that it is not easy to state a convincing alternative to the dogmatic Catholic claim. And we can further recognize that there is in Catholicism an understanding of the Christian community as a source of moral insight which our modern individualistic Protestantism needs to recognize more fully, though it can find a corrective in its own heritage.[9]

Protestants hold the Roman Catholic answer will not do; and for two reasons. The first is that a human institution subject to all the sins and errors of mortality is here absolutized as the infallible spokesman for God. This means that the freedom of God to speak a new word through the prophet, a word against the Church is denied. Thus Catholicism rejects one of the cardinal truths which is given in the revelation of God out of which the Bible came. God in His freedom raises up men who speak His word of judgment against all "holy" orders and institutions. When this ultimate religious reservation which prevents our identifying any human ethic with the absolute will of God is not made, the evil of absolutizing some relative tradition or standpoint begins to manifest itself. It is clear in the history of Catholicism that its moral teaching embodies and sanctifies the relative social and cultural values of those civilizations in which the Church was formed and in which it has lived. We read in a Catholic book of moral theology the following:

Holy Scripture teaches that while men and women are united by God in a most intimate union, woman is not man's equal, but his helpmate and companion. It follows that woman in public and social life may legitimately aspire to no other role than that of a true helpmate to man.

We know quite well that we are not listening here to the voice of God.[10] We are listening to the voice of the dominant class in a feudal society.[11] The Catholic ethic is a frozen ethic. It moves glacierlike through human history, carrying with it the debris of outworn values and stubbornly trying to break through everything in its path by the sheer weight of its dogmatic claim. The absurd position of the Roman Church on birth control is a striking and pitiful example.[12]

The other failure of the Catholic solution is that the basic moral dilemma remains unsolved. Neither the individual Catholic, whether lay or religious, nor the Church itself, escapes the ambiguities of the moral situation. The Church does evil as well as good. In spite of the heroic renunciation of the religious orders they live in the world, depend upon it, and become entangled with its economic and political injustices.[13] What actually takes place in the Catholic attempt to meet the relativities of moral choices is a continuous compromise with principles to fit situations. An example is afforded by the attempt to say what is fair and unfair in war. Says the teaching of the Church:

> Absolutely damnable and illicit means of warfare are: lying, perjury, the intentional dissemination of false reports, e.g. of faked victories. Among the licit means are: espionage, stratagems, ambuscades, etc.; these are allowed because they are not based on lies pure and simple, but merely furnish the enemy an occasion for drawing false conclusions.[14]

Certainly we must recognize the importance of the attempt to keep the moral sense alive even in war, but this method which seeks to distinguish always between a "right" and a "wrong" tends toward the subtle hypocrisy of self-justification. Some reason must always be found why our act is right and another's wrong. The depth of the moral problem which was confessed in the Christian News Letter during the last war is not recognized: "As the war takes its course the contradictions between its necessities and the Christian purpose deepens."[15]

III

Protestantism came into being through a new understanding of what it means to live as a Christian in the world. The Reformers saw that the basis of moral responsibility and decision of the Christian does not lie in the elaboration of principles but in the concrete response of free men to the call of God, which is a call to action and service. That is our vocation. It was this doctrine with which the Reformers pried Christian ethics loose from the dominion of the Church. It was this by which they broke the distinction between the religious and the secular orders. It was here they discovered a foundation for ethics which transcends all legalistic systems. And it was this doctrine, in turn based on the doctrine of justification by faith, which made it possible for Luther and Calvin to say what it means to live the Christian life of service to the God of love in the midst of the tragic necessities of this world.[16]

Though the Reformers laid the basis for the life of moral responsibility, they did not carry through the full implications of the new conception of vocation. How and why this failure came about is the familiar story, told most fully in the studies of Weber and Tawney.[17] The doctrine of vocation became the means of sanctifying the emerging values of capitalist society. Success in business was taken as a mark of divine election. Lutheran ethics, following certain tendencies in Luther's own thought but neglecting his main intention, conceived the social orders outside the Church as necessary bulwarks against sin, but obeying principles of a different order from the demands of the Gospel of love. Today with the increasing secularization of our society, the word "vocation" has almost lost any religious connotation. It simply means to most people the way in which anyone earns his living.

It may be the word "vocation" is beyond recovery, though its roots are in the New Testament. But the *meaning* of the word which the Reformers saved for Christianity must be recovered. It is the key to the ethical profundity and power of the Gospel. Its essence is that what we have to do as moral agents is determined by the fact that we serve in this world the living God who is our Creator and Redeemer. With that insight we must reconceive the Christian understanding of the moral demand in every social relationship from the family to the world community. It is a tremendous task; but there has already been a substantial beginning upon it.

Two Protestant theologians have recently given us major discussions of the doctrine of vocation in relation to Protestant ethics. One is Dr. Robert L. Calhoun in *God and the Common Life*, and the other is Dr. Emil Brunner in *The Divine Imperative*.[18] It is instructive to examine these side by side, not only because both contain such great merits, but because taken together they strongly suggest that neither Calhoun's liberalism nor Brunner's neo-orthodoxy gives a wholly satisfactory foundation to the doctrine of vocation. We may be encouraged to try again.

In Calhoun's work, God is interpreted as the world-maker who intelligently and persuasively works to bring man toward fulfillment. Man's call from God is to see what God is doing and to share in the labor. "To do needful work, then, to lose oneself and find oneself therein, to participate thus in a common task and a shared life: this and the summons to it, we shall mean by vocation."[19] Here the focus of attention is upon vocation as work, rather than upon the total ethical obligation. Yet even with this legitimate narrowing of the emphasis Calhoun does not bring sharply into view the problem of moral action in a sinful world. He rightly argues that we do not need to surrender belief in the possibility of progress while we discard the notion of its inevitability. He makes necessary reservations about the eternal tension between perfection and the limitations of human achievement.[20] But the problem of choice between evils is somewhat by-passed. For example, writing as he did in the midst of the depression (1935), Calhoun discusses the problem of revolutionary violence as a means to correction of economic injustices. He does not reject the possible necessity of violence, but he says: "One must weigh coldly the chances that the proper group will get into power."[21] That is a sensible statement; but it does not help us to interpret

these situations into which we are "hurled" by the irrational circumstances of life. There are eruptions of violence in which we
either participate or renounce responsibility. These difficulties have
been stressed by Professor Calhoun in his later writing; and one
can believe that were he to restate the doctrine of vocation today
it would be put in the context of a sterner view of the historical
realities.[22]

In contrast to the liberal view the doctrine of the universal fact
of sin as the context of moral decision forms the substance of
Brunner's doctrine of vocation. For him the notion of the calling
is the solution of the problem of the Christian service of God in a
sinful world. The calling, Brunner makes clear, is not only that
situation in which we work; but it is that divine summons which
comes to us where we are and in obedience to which we find the
meaning of life. Brunner says:

> This idea of Calling is full of eschatological tension and a daring which
> conquers the world; indeed we might almost call it a 'divine audacity' and
> the reason is this: God takes over all responsibility for our action in the
> world which in itself is sinful, if we, on our part, will only do here and now
> that which the present situation demands from one who loves God and
> his neighbor.[23]

I have already stated one qualification which I believe needs to
be made of Brunner's doctrine.[24] The statement that the world "in
itself is sinful" leaves inadequate place for the continuing bond
between creation and the love of God. Some of the circumstances
which Brunner regards as the consequence of sin are simply natural
and necessary conditions for the growth of life in love. A further
problem in Brunner's thought is that his doctrine is bound up with
a conception of Providence in which the irrational circumstances
of life, that is, our finding ourselves in this time and place and situation, are too simply identified with the inscrutable purposes of
God.[25] He makes too little room for the notion which is so well
stated by Calhoun and which surely belongs in the Christian view

of life, that the world is an unfinished world. Its structures and processes are pliable in the hands of the creative God, and in some measure, in the hands of His creatures. When the doctrine of Providence is given a deterministic interpretation the notion of "calling" can too easily be used to justify the particular class structure in which we find ourselves.[26]

IV

These two contributions have opened the way for a rediscovery of the meaning of the Christian life as a life of moral integrity in devotion to the will of God. The Christian ethic can cope with the realistic situation of life in a history riddled with evil. It will be an ethic which interprets the moral life as the whole response of man to the demand of God, not merely a legalistic obedience to abstract principles. Yet it will be an ethic which holds in creative balance the authority of enduring moral principles with the freedom of the Christian spirit.

The clue to ethical reconstruction is this: *The living God whose nature and purpose is love calls us to respond in our freedom to the tasks which are set for us by the fact that He is at work in our human history both as Creator and as Redeemer.*

It is perhaps futile to speculate upon what might have happened if the doctrine of vocation had been thus understood from the beginning. The text which has been made the basis of traditional formulations is, of course, Paul's statement: "Let each man abide in that calling wherein he was called."[27] We may note the problem of Paul's exact meaning here has never been solved. It would be going too far to say that clarification of the wording of a text could alone have altered Christian history; but we may be allowed to speculate upon what might have been made of the doctrine of calling if Paul's statement had been interpreted in the light of his full teaching. Suppose, for example, the definition of the call had been always understood in relation to Romans 12. "I beseech you therefore brethren that you present your bodies a living sacrifice, holy, acceptable to God which is your reasonable service." Here the call of God is a summons to the new life of service. We escape the pernicious notion that we must regard as divinely given and unalterable the social status into which men happen to be born.

The true New Testament sense of the calling does not put the emphasis on the social status or rank of the Christian. It means that the Christian wherever he is has been called out by God to become a member of the *new* community, the Body of Christ in the world. To put this interpretation of the meaning of vocation into a formal statement:

The divine call to us men, and our response to it, means that we are responsible for doing here and now in the situation in which we stand whatever will serve the work of God who is seeking to bring all life to fulfillment in that universal community of love which is the real good of every creature.

To do here and now what needs to be done for the sake of the real good, is the substance of the Christian acknowledgment of our moral obligation. The freedom of the Christian man which Luther rewon for the Christian is that which comes from seeing that no arbitrary rule, ecclesiastical law, or abstract principle takes precedence over this concrete necessity and our conscientious response to it. "What needs to be done" is to serve the good which God is bringing about. What God is doing must be seen partly under the aspect of creation and partly under that of redemption. That is why love has its tragic work as well as its joyous work. Every ethical decision must be made not only in the light of the high possibilities for good which we envision, but also in the light of what is possible in the actual situation. One of the burdens which love assumes is that of reckoning with the grim necessities. Once this truth is understood a new light is thrown on the moral problem.

Christian love is not primarily a matter of kindly personal affections. It is a matter of responsible action to serve the good of life. The degree to which the Christian teaching of love has been shoved aside as irrelevant because this has not been understood is well illustrated by the remark of a student of American relations with Central America in a recent volume on American foreign policy. Mr. Allen Haden says:

In this wonderland of rhetoric the Good Neighbor Policy has unfortunately become confused with the Christian principle of loving one's neighbor. But the question is not whether we love the Cubans or the Cubans love us. The question is whether the United States will consume so much Cuban sugar, alcohol, and bagass that Cuban canefield peons will have work and Cuban politics, in consequence, will stay attuned to Washington and not feel forced to find political friends elsewhere in order to sell sugar.

The question is not whether we love Costa Riquenos, Guatemaltecos, or Nicaraguenses. The question is whether United States government policy reinforces or mitigates absentee banana land-lordism, whose agents manipulate Central American politics, banking, and general income.[28]

It may well be that the forces which will actually decide this question will operate in terms of interests and attitudes which have nothing to do with Christian love. But to any Christian who has responsibility in such a situation, what he is to do about it has everything to do with whether or not he loves his neighbor. Love is nothing if it is not the will to justice, and, beyond justice, the will to the opening of the way for a new community of mind and spirit. Whatever can be done about absentee-landlordism to serve those ends can be done as an expression of Christian love.

There are compromises involved in every political decision. But if a choice between evils is to have any moral meaning at all, one evil will be judged less than another because it involves less destruction of some real good. Archbishop Temple clearly recognizes the moral problem of Christian politics: "The art of government is not to devise what would be the best system for saints to work, but to secure that the lower motives actually found among men prompt that conduct which the higher motives demand. The law which associates imprisonment with theft leads a dishonest or defectively honest man to act honestly."[29] But the Archbishop never allows us to forget that the Christian's motivation involves more than a calculated prudence. It involves the obligation to find ways in which through political action the higher motives may be released and the higher community may be given opportunity to grow.

If there be a place for the assumption of the moral risks of compromise in the way of love, there is also place for renunciation which involves radical attack on everything which stands in the way of the new order which God wills. The spirit of love emerges in every Christian generation as a demand that men defy the claims of some particular state or church, and refuse to participate in some evil order. It sometimes leads Christians to the sacrifice of all privilege in order to share life with the lowliest and neediest of mankind. It sometimes involves the giving of life itself that God's work may be done. There are the lives of Schweitzer and Damien and Kagawa in which the purity and heroism of renunciation of comfort and privilege forever humble us and reveal our shallowness. Yet I do not believe the conclusion is justified that the only Christian life is that in which family, privileged profession, and public responsibility are renounced. The work of God depends in part upon men of loyalty and devotion in the places of public power. The test is whether that power is used in responsible service to the God who is moving against the injustices in the present structures of power. In such a world each one of us has to make his Christian way.

We see, then, why Protestant ethics does not attempt to say legalistically what is right and wrong for every man. It is in the responsible spirit of love to God and our neighbor that we must decide concretely what is right or wrong. This is how we understand that moral radicalism which begins in the greatest of the Hebrew prophets and which has run through Christian ethics from the beginning. The prophets asserted the demand of the clean heart against all the specific requirements of the law.[30] Jesus summed up all the law in the two commandments to love God and our neighbor.[31] Paul puts it radically when he says, "All things are lawful for me; but all things edify not."[32] It is in the actual service of my neighbor's need and my own that the ultimate permission or prohibition of any action lies. St. Augustine put the Christian position most strikingly, "Love, and then do as you will."[33]

V

It might appear that the problems of Christian ethics can be solved at one stroke. The Gospel supersedes all law. The one thing needful is our response to the call of God. But the experience of Christianity proves we cannot stop at this point. We cannot dispense with the moral law, either in its basic formal principles or the multitude of rules and precepts which follow from them. But in Protestant ethics we understand these in a new way. They are no longer injunctions which have to be applied legalistically to every situation; they are guides to the meaning of responsibility, that is, to our vocation. What this means we must analyze in relation to "the law of love" which is the fundamental moral principle, and then in relation to those other principles and precepts which are endlessly multiplied and elaborated in human living.

The "law of love" has a peculiar character as law. Its peculiarity consists in the fact that as a law it commands the spirit of love which must be something more than obedience to law. The relevance of this to our analysis of community as the principle of the real good can be made clear. For "community" as that order which is sought by love can be stated as a formal principle. It is the order in which the members of a society are so related that the freedom, uniqueness, and power of each serves the freedom, uniqueness, and growth of all the other members. But growth of community is not merely a formal principle, it is an actual process in the world. To use an analogy, the mathematical statement of the position in the spectrum of the color blue is the abstract definition of the color; but to know the color blue as it is in nature one must see it with his eyes. So the law of love which is the requirement of community is a law which can be formally stated as a principle of action; but community must be experienced in life before we can really say we know what it is. Moral action in response to the divine call is not simply a matter of applying the law of love to a situation. It means sharing in the creation of a community of good in existence. That is a living process. The law of love or community, then, is not bondage for the spirit, but the dynamic rational principle which can guide the spirit in its service of the real good.

The law of love, however, must be supplemented. We might imagine a person so attuned to the needs of his neighbor, and so lacking in sinful self-will that he would spontaneously see what needed to be done and do it. But so long as we are not in this state of perfection we have to live by the rational elaboration of moral principles, and by specific moral and legal rules: "Thou shalt not kill." "Thou shalt not commit adultery." "No man shall be deprived of life, liberty, or property without due process of law." When we set the freedom of the Christian above all law, we do not discard such injunctions.

We regard moral principles in a new light. They are more or less adequate guides to responsible action. The one absolute demand is that we serve the growth of community. But we have to seek community through an endless variety of circumstances and in a world which often does not permit us to seek it directly. Take an example of the specific command, "Thou shalt not kill." If we make that an absolute rule we can make no sense of it. It cannot mean to kill no living thing; for all life must kill. We kill bacteria which attack us. We kill plants and animals for food. There are circumstances in which nearly every one of us would admit the necessity of killing another human being. Your failure to kill a madman running amok may permit him to kill a dozen innocent people. Consider the suicides of Jews and others in Germany who either had to take their own lives and those of their families or have them taken in far more horrible fashion. Try to solve the moral problem by absolutizing a command like this and you make it hopeless. But take "thou shalt not kill" as a statement of the obligation of all life to serve the good of all, and you understand it in a new way. Every life is sacred. It has its place in the economy of God. We take it justifiably only for the sake of the whole community of life.

We may use another illustration from philosophical ethics. Consider Kant's principle: "Act as if the maxim of your action were by your will to become a universal law of nature."[34] The attempt to make this the basis of all moral judgments lands in endless difficulties. It is purely formal. It takes no account of the differences of individual circumstances. But consider the maxim an expression of the meaning of responsibility and it comes suddenly to life. It means you are only one among many, you cannot act without reference to the whole. You cannot claim superior status or special exemptions from the universal moral obligation. The moral obligation upon you is the same for each one. This is, I believe, the actual movement of Kant's thought, though it is obscured by his formalism. The real content of his principle is dependent upon the Christian apprehension of the mutual obligation of all rational beings to the real good of one universal society.

In addition to moral principles we have to look at human experience for moral guidance. This raises the complex problems of the "orders"—family, state, economic—and their relations to natural law theories of ethics. It is not to our purpose here to invade this complex field. What we are suggesting is that the ethical problem must be viewed from the standpoint of the dynamic relationship between man's experience and God's working. It is the static character of the doctrines of the orders and of natural law theories which is their limitation. Emil Brunner is entirely right in his criticism of contemporary theologies which have tried "to deduce the order of law and the state from the historical event Christ, the cross of Christ. How fantastic the deduction is must be plain to any unprejudiced mind."[35] There is no substitute in Christian ethics for a continual attempt to relate the good which we know in Christ to the full circumstances of life as these are disclosed in our experience with the best scientific, historical, and other data we can get. The family, for example, belongs to the order of creation. Mutual responsibilities are created for each member by the biological and psychological facts of our nature as sexual beings dependent upon one another. But the question of what form of the family will most fully release the freedom and capabilities of its members and sustain the growth of the most intimate and full community of persons cannot be answered dogmatically out of the religious tradition. All the orders of creation are in process. They are all subject to indeterminate modification. The service of God involves both the profoundest respect for the way in which the orders serve justice and mutuality in any given situation, and a continual attempt to find where they block the fuller community of life with life. The call to adjust our human ways to the demands of new good is as truly a part of the Christian vocation as is the call to maintain the abiding values in the orders which sustain and guide us. The doctrine of vocation thus transcends both the conservative and progressive attitudes. It requires both. A Church in which this approach to ethics is understood will be more fully able to reconcile within its own body those who emphasize one or the other principle, and those who disagree profoundly in their judgment on particular moral issues.

The two intolerable positions are: first, one which deals irresponsibly with the given structures of society, as if some ultimate perfection could be secured by human effort; and, second, one which merely says the world is full of evils, "you can't change human nature," and hence accepts the status quo.

How shall the Christian find his concrete duty and service where he is? Every statement of ethical theory is incomplete until that question has been faced. Since as Protestants we hold that the call of God has to be understood and appropriated by the individual in his own conscience, we cannot prescribe some legalistic method by which moral decisions can be made. Conscience stands above church, and above advice and counsel. This is a real loneliness and "forsakenness" in the experience of moral decisions in which we literally take our lives into our own hands. Nothing less than this is the meaning of Protestant freedom.

Once we are clear that nothing can destroy this freedom, we can say where our resources are. In the first place, we have something to learn from the Catholic emphasis in ethics. We are not just individuals. We are members of a community, the Church. There is a pinnacle of freedom in the individual conscience, but in large measure our conscience itself is a social product. We have the best chance of hearing the Word of God to us as individuals when our lives are deeply rooted in the religious community through which the sensitizing of conscience takes place. This community is not only the particular church group to which we belong, but the whole living body of those who in all times have sought God and been found by Him. The fact that we do not finally submit our consciences to the dictates of any tradition or institution is the best possible reason for using our freedom to appropriate the moral wisdom of all traditions and institutions. The fact of freedom makes the more necessary the sharing of life with that company of people whose faith and moral conviction are necessary to each individual's moral sanity.

Our second resource in making moral decisions is prayer. There is no way to the deeper levels of moral insight more important than the lifting of the mind and conscience to the spirit of God. The

humble act of self-examination; the opening of the closed self to
the cleansing and healing work of God; the sealing of moral resolve
in dependence upon the power of God; all this is what real prayer
can mean in the moral life. Divine guidance does not mean the in-
sertion by supernatural means of ideas in our minds. It is dangerous
to take any particular notion which we derive in the moment of
prayer and identify it with the will of God. We know too much
about the ways of self-deception and wish-fulfillment to be satisfied
with that. Dr. Buttrick in a classic phrase has said that the greatest
service of prayer is "the courageous and creative acceptance of the
terms of mortal life."[36] One of those terms is the fallibility of human
decisions. Prayer is the sword of the spirit even against its own evil.
It is most effective when we approach it in the humility of confession that God's mercy is our first and last need. Then guidance
does come in illumination and the power of resolve.

There is one further resource for the Christian life. God is at
work in history. He calls us to respond in action. It is true, therefore, that we discover our moral responsibility as we begin to act
responsibly. The truth, "He that doeth the will shall know of the
doctrine," can be distorted into a false pragmatism.[37] Action alone
does not reveal truth. But there is wisdom here. The way we come
to know our calling is to begin to respond to God's demand, where
we are, however feebly and uncertainly. The final word which the
Protestant sermon must ever address to him who would discover
God is: begin to live where you are as if you knew what responsibility meant. Take your neighbor seriously. See him in Christ. Move
out toward him in love, and the miracle will happen. You will
begin to learn how God can use your life. To him who does what
he can will be given light.

The Christian conception of the moral life as service in the world
of the order of good which is never wholly realized in the world
opens the way to moral integrity. Belief in integrity is possible if
we can be freed of two illusions. One is that the world order is

fixed and there is nothing original ever to be done within its broken state. The other is that we can find some way of life which involves no moral perplexities, and in which we can regard ourselves as free from sin. To identify what we are doing with what God is doing is the open sesame to fanaticism. The true spirituality of John Wesley is revealed not by his teaching that perfection is possible in the Christian life but in the fact that he never claimed perfection for himself. Integrity is possible not because we can be altogether what we ought to be, but because we can participate in the working of God whose grace includes forgiveness for what we are. Justification by faith in God's grace is the ultimate relationship within which such moral achievement as is possible for us will always have its rightful place.

What kind of human society then can we legitimately work for and hope for?

CHAPTER SEVEN

The Good Earth and the Good Society

THE hope for a "better world" of human dignity, productive peace, and social justice formed a cardinal tenet of the liberal expression of Christian faith. We are all beginning to learn that Christian hope ought never to be expressed as a prediction of the course of history. We cannot demand that the future be bent to conform to human plans. Christian hope is the spirit in which we accept the risk of the future. We move into the unknown with faith and expectancy because we have seen salvation accomplished in the midst of evil.

At this time when hope runs low among men, we should be ready to give as sane an interpretation as we can fashion of the possibilities of human life. Christianity would be a sorry failure today if it kept itself aloof from the search for constructive solutions of human problems. Secular idealism may not reach the height of religious faith, but a conscientious effort to bring a better order into the world is one of the continuing signs of the image of God in man.

I

We need to consider what kind of hope for the better world is implied in the viewpoint we have developed and show how we must hold this hope in strict balance with a Christian realism concerning the evil which is within us and about us. We need to formulate the Christian hope in a way which embraces what is valid in both realism and utopianism.

I use the word "utopianism" deliberately because it brings us straightway to the crux of our problem. The word "utopian" is usually hissed rather than spoken today. It is hurled with reproach at liberal Christianity which is charged with having allowed the Christian faith to be replaced by a secular utopianism. The American approach to politics and history is characterized as "utopian" when critics wish to say that Americans do not understand historical realities. Richard Niebuhr describes this dissolution of the Gospel in American Christianity: "A God without wrath brought men without sin into a Kingdom without judgment through the ministrations of a Christ without a cross."[1]

We have admitted the justice in this criticism. We want no return to a view of history which deals superficially with the fact of evil. It may serve the purpose of clarity if having made this qualification I state bluntly my thesis that the utopianism in the liberal faith had a lasting value which it derived partly from the Christian faith and partly from what was valid in the world view of the Enlightenment. We could make no greater mistake today than to allow this utopian element to be uprooted from our Christian experience and witness. Utopianism rightly understood has a place in the Christian response to life.

To use the term "utopian" merely as a scornful epithet does not serve the purpose of clear thinking. Let us ask what it means. What is utopian in a bad sense and what is not?

In the narrow sense of the word "a Utopia" is an imaginative picture of a perfect order of life, projected either backward toward a golden age or forward into an ideal future. From Plato's *Republic* to the several visions of H. G. Wells, the Utopias have served as the vehicles for the expression of wisdom about life, social preachment, and sheer imaginative delight. Culturally speaking, at least, we should be much the poorer without them.

It is doubtful if any one generalization about the functions and significance of these artistic and intellectual visions can be made.

Mr. Toynbee is probably oversimplifying when he says that their primary intent has been to arrest the process of the decay of civilization by trying to show that certain selected elements of the civilization are essential to perfection. Plato, for example, borrows some of the Spartan ideals for his perfect state in order to arrest the decay of Athens.[2] This misses, I believe, the profounder significance of Plato's *Republic* as an expression of philosophical wisdom. A strong case has been made by F. J. E. Woodbridge that Plato not only does not seriously regard his "perfect state" as realizable, but that he means to make us see the error of imposing perfection too rigorously on human fallibility.[3] Edward Bellamy's *Looking Backward* illustrates the utopia which becames a persuasive call to radical social reform.[4] It also illustrates one of the functions of utopian thought as a medium of realistic criticism of the present. When Bellamy says that in his new society the editors of newspapers are elected by the subscribers, he hits straight at the problem of the democratic control of the sources of propaganda which has become critical for us.

The religious utopianism of the Anabaptists in the Reformation period and of the Levellers and Diggers in England grew out of the Christian expectation of the imminent end of the world and the attempt within the religious community to begin to live the life of the new order here and now. The modern utopias of liberalism and of Marxism have asserted the possibility of the order which overcomes evil emerging either through gradual development or catastrophic struggles in history. Both Marxists and liberals who expect in their different ways the coming of the good society are able to live in a kind of anticipatory participation in the perfection of the goal. Its triumph is assured. A Condorcet predicting the age of peace from his prison during the French Revolution, or the German Communist in a Nazi concentration camp, may live through the trials of the present with a serenity born of the knowledge that what ought to be will be.

The "utopian" experimental societies so familiar in American history have drawn little groups of people into the adventure of proving that the new order is possible. They all failed; yet many were splendid failures and released into the mainstream of our culture forces and ideals which we would not willingly let go.[5]

This cursory survey reminds us that the "lure of perfection" has its own power, and appears as a recurring phenomenon among sensitive souls. Our capacity to deal with what we call the realistic problems of life would be weakened without this element which contains something profound in spite of the romantic and even absurd ways in which it may be expressed.

We are encouraged to look for the deeper element in utopianism through the labors of the sociologist Karl Mannheim, who has characterized it in a brilliant manner. If we follow Mannheim we are able to identify a general meaning of "utopianism" as one of the ways in which groups in history take hold of their historical situation.

Mannheim describes the "utopian mentality" in these words: "Every age allows to arise . . . those ideas and values in which are contained in condensed form the unrealized and the unfulfilled tendencies which represent the needs of each age. These intellectual elements then become the explosive material for bursting the limits of the existing order."[6] The utopian element appears where men believe in the creative eruption of forces which are capable of meeting the new demands of life. Now we begin to see one aspect of the historical significance of the Christian faith that God is powerful and that He will act. Mannheim himself traces the "spiritualiza-tion" of politics in modern culture to its origin in the chiliastic utopias of exploited and oppressed Christian groups which began to try to make radical changes in the political order.[7] Faith that God's power was producing the new order became a call to revo-lutionary human response. Religion which has not lost its utopian-ism is the opposite of the opiate of the people.

The sense in which the utopian element belongs in the Christian view of history now becomes clear. It does not require the assertion that perfection is possible in any life or society. It does mean that history is open to the power of God and through His power society can be transformed in the direction of the real good. It is one of the functions of theology to be a critic of utopias and utopianism. Criticism is evaluation. The Christian mind will seek at all times for the possibility of new good which may be hidden from our sight, but which we know is everywhere present.

Utopianism in the Christian hope is that spirit which knows that man is never satisfied or at peace until he discovers the meaning of life in the community of love with God and his fellows. It is the everlasting expectancy of God's mercy sustaining and redeeming our twisted lives. It is the willingness to trust life to Him even when we cannot see the way through. It is the willingness to let the old order be shaken to pieces and to believe that a better is possible under God who is forever making "a new heaven and a new earth." This expectancy of the Christian spirit has more than one mode of expression. It may release a zestful activism in which we start out to get things done. But there is also a brooding and silent patience in the face of disaster, when we see no way to turn and nothing we can do. But the waiting can be filled with hope for him who believes that God keeps His own watch in the night.

Hope itself is born of the spirit's grip upon ultimate things. The forms of hope are functions of the world view of a particular mind or culture. When we try to say what we hope for and why we hope, we begin and end with the vision of God as the source and meaning of life. But we also point to the life about us and try to say what we see in it that sustains our hope. When we do this we discover that Christian hope has many dimensions. We shall explore three of them.

II

1. *Christian hope is sustained by, and expresses itself in, a reverent grateful love for the good earth.*

In asserting the goodness of our natural environment we should avoid a false sentimentality. There is a mystery of evil in the creation. Human life is often crushed, starved, or killed by disease before its "natural" course is run. Yet amidst the travail of creation there is the fact of the tender nurture of life. The earth is but a passing order. Still if this present cosmos is but a wasting flow of energy, in faith we believe that creative love will go on doing its patient work. God is not bound to one universe or one cosmic epoch, and His work is manifest in this order which sustains our life. The prayer for "our daily bread" is the acknowledgment of our dependence, and the expression of hope that the God who has given life will continue to give it. We experience His grace in the order of the stars and seasons, the rhythm of work and rest, the repeated miracle of birth, growth, death, and new life. The Christian attitude permits no ultimate asceticism toward the things of earth and sense. When the meek shall inherit the earth their reward is like the reward of the Kingdom of heaven itself.

We acknowledge that the criticism of romantic tendencies in the theologies which have stressed the immanence of God is often justified. We are not defending the sweetish sentiments taught in much poetry and song which discreetly ignore the cruel and darker side of nature. But there is more than sentimentality in a reverent acceptance of this life with fear of its evil and love for its good. Such acceptance comes from the discovery of the patient working of God as He bears us with Him into the future. As Tagore wrote: "Every child comes into the world with the message that God does not yet despair of man."[8]

Even death has its place in the service of God. It is the way life makes way for more life.[9] Death establishes a common fate for every living thing, and thus gives a decisive character to our dependence upon God and our unity with all His creatures. It opens the way to the participation of this finite life in the infinite life of God. The traditional doctrine that death is in the world as the result of sin may easily lead to confusion. Death as separation from God is the mark of sin. But death as a natural fact is one of the conditions under which God's work gets done. Here is a decisive point at which we need to recognize that our existence as finite creatures offers us something more than temptations to sin. The theologies which stress original sin inordinately tend to see nothing but temptation in the natural order. But there are also persuasions to love in our creaturely experience. Even in death God draws us to Himself.

The reverent acceptance of the natural conditions of life has practical consequences. When man regards nature only as something to be exploited for immediate gain without concern for the whole good it is meant to serve, he loses even his capacity to make full use of nature. A scientific conquest of nature without the sense of reverence will always turn against us. Mind becomes calculating, practical, sure of its capacity to dominate. Yet this imperial confidence of man the exploiter has nothing to serve. It loses the zest of life. It has no power to see it whole. That is much of what is wrong with man's spirit today. Sheer control over life for the sake of control is self-defeating. The good earth is good only as we love it in the using of it.

The Malvern conference of English churchmen said in 1941, "We must recover reverence for the earth and its resources, treating it no longer as a reservoir of potential wealth to be exploited but as a storehouse of divine bounty on which we utterly depend."[10] Mr. David Lilienthal has given practical evidence of the validity of this religious attitude in his account of how the principle of the "respect for the unity of nature" emerged in the development of the Tennessee Valley Authority. The principle is that soil, forests, rivers, and our technical skill will together serve human life provided we understand and respect the interrelatedness of all life. Thought- less exploitation of one natural resource without taking account of the whole restorative cycle of nature and the whole need of man wastes natural wealth. Mr. Lilienthal gives the striking example of Ducktown, Tennessee. To this town came a copper mining company interested apparently only in copper. To get fuel for the smelter furnaces the magnificent hard wood forests were cut down. Fumes from the smelter laid their killing blight on the remaining vegeta- tion. Rainfall washed away the good soil now unprotected. Man made a desert of the land.[11] The actual cost in natural wealth of this one failure is staggering. Today new technical skill has rendered the smelter fumes harmless. A program is under way to restore the lost forests and fields. The earth will yield her increase when man respects her laws. As the engineer describes the principle of the unity of nature an ancient word takes on new meaning, "The earth is the Lord's and the fullness thereof." God made us members not only of one another, but of the one great society of all creatures.

It may be held that our earth really provides only meager living for most human beings. One school of economists suggests that nothing much better than poverty for the masses of men is con- ceivable within the economy of nature as we know it. Certainly it is true that we cannot expect, and indeed we would not want, a world which did not call forth a strenuous disciplined effort of mind and body for the maintenance of life. Yet the burden of grinding poverty destroys the possibility of the full life for the masses of men. The scientist, K. F. Mather, has made out a strong case that there is "Enough and to Spare" of natural resources. The resources are in the earth and the means to use those resources are at hand to lift mankind beyond the threat of starvation, and out of the grinding condition of insecure physical existence. Fairfield Osborn in *Our Plundered Planet* gives a less optimistic analysis, but makes the same argument that intelligent planning is imperative for the full use of the resources we have.[12] Advances in medical science are so dramatic we need only to mention them. Life expectancy in America has doubled since 1900. That is a gain for human good beyond calculation. Scientific resources for dealing with mental illness are increasing. While our culture produces neurotic personalities, we know some of the causes and some of the ways by which men can be helped to accept life and to live it with adequacy rather than to be broken by it. All this takes human effort and ingenuity. Nature does not give her bounty without human labor. But man did not invent his own inventiveness. That itself is a gift of grace.

Christian faith accepts the challenge of the natural environment to make it serve human fulfillment. We need to make certain that neither the mood of despair of our time, nor the theological concentration of attention on man as sinner robs us of a respect for life's essential goodness and the importance of intelligence and disciplined effort in meeting the particular problems which are set for us by the conditions of human existence. Hope for man is reborn whenever we rediscover our dependence upon the good earth. That hope will be expressed in a reverent concern that what God has provided shall be used to serve nothing less than His good which is the one real good of all things.

2. *The Christian hope for man is sustained by, and expressed in, the never-ending struggle for the Good Society.*

"The Good Society" is a utopian symbol. That is its power. The hope for a redeemed humanity, living in dignity, freedom, and brotherhood under God is an integral part of the Christian faith about the meaning of the human adventure. Whatever blocks the coming of the Good Society is an enemy of Christ. What helps humanity forward toward that society is proof that Christ reigns with power. This hope for the Good Society was justified in liberal theology both by its ultimate faith in God and by what it took to be experiences of real victory over evil.

We can save that hope. We must save it if Christianity is to have an ethical gospel for human affairs. The ethic of love presupposes that in some measure what ought to be can come to be. Such is the radical faith with which the Christian spirit ought to release us to tackle our social problems.

We now know that it is imperative for us to recognize that the Christian hope for the Good Society can be saved only if we achieve a new formulation of it. We know that something was wrong with the optimism of the social gospel. What is not so clear is how to bring the spiritual and moral depth of that gospel into a new philosophy of Christian action in history. But a most promising solution is emerging in the theological discussion today. The key is this: The aim of Christian social ethics is to discover and promote the establishment of those conditions which will aid the growth of communities of freedom, justice, and equality. These communities will not be "the great community," but they will support that community, and be something like it. We cannot directly create a good society. It must grow. No growth is mechanical or wholly controllable even in the lowest orders of life. At the human level the growth of community depends on the free response of men to the needs of their neighbors. What we can do is to discover in human experience those social, economic, political, and cultural conditions which may open the way for the life of free men under God.

To make clear what is new in this approach to the social gospel let us take the analogy of the family. Suppose a man and a woman marry, and set out to establish the Perfect Marriage. They determine to govern the whole of life toward the full realization of the ideal. They manage their children's lives with the intention of seeing to it that nothing but the most perfect domestic order is established. Now we quickly sense there is something dangerous and humanly intolerable in such an effort. It has been well said, when we work at our virtues they may become deadly. We are forcing something which cannot be forced. When our try for perfection falls short as it must, we have no resources with which to meet it, if we have staked the meaning of life on achieving nothing less than the ideal.

Some forms of the Christian attack on the social problem have expressed just such a taut idealism. Men set out to create their ideal Christian order of life, that is, to control history.

Whatever the moral heroism it may elicit the limitations of this idealistic approach are now clear. The structure of the ideal society cannot be finally prescribed, nor can we directly create a new order. The stuff of human history and human nature simply does not permit that kind of attack. We have to make our way through monstrous evil, and make endless concessions to what is actually there in the forces which shape our destiny. The crucial difference between two ways of looking at human problems is the difference between trying to manage history according to plan, and a responsible planning within a history which is more successfully dealt with when we recognize the unmanageable factors within it.

We can know in principle for all situations that some structures of human society block the real good, and some may open the way for it. Here, then, is the distinctive task of Christian social philosophy: to raise in every social order the question, "What is its consequence for the community of mutuality among men?" There is, for example, no Christian economics in the sense of a distinctive Christian science of economic behavior, nor any one Christian answer to the question, "What is a good economic order?" But there is a Christian question to put to all economic orders and programs. What does this way of life do to the freedom, equality, and growth of mutuality of the people who live in it?

In the elaboration of this approach to social ethics Christians should remember that while they have a distinctive witness they have no monopoly of the insights and knowledge which are required. There will always be differences of judgment in the Christian group on specific political and social issues. I am here concerned to state a method of approach to the problem rather than to discuss the complex issues which surround us everywhere. But "a moral discussion is inconclusive and even trivial, if it leaves out the question of its application," as Gregory Vlastos has said.[13] In order to be as specific as possible about this approach to Christian social philosophy I shall outline in arbitrary fashion five general principles which I suggest can be supported by the evidence of human experience as being necessary guides to the conditions under which the Good Society can grow.

First, the resources of the good earth and of human intelligence must provide for every responsible member of society the minimal basis for decent health, housing, education, and recreation. We have come very near to accepting this charge on the total social body in principle, though we are a long way from achieving it in practice. The problem in America is not primarily one of wealth. There is enough. The real problems arise in finding the adequate ways to provide and distribute such security. Ways are being found. If one rides the downtown bus in one of our large cities through the slum areas in which children play in dirty alleys behind saloons, and then passes a housing project with clean, sunlit yards, and children playing in safety, he can only say, "So far, so good, not only for them but for all society." The fundamental securities, basic education, and the necessities of healthful and wholesome life can be shared among all.

Second, political institutions must be found which unite stable order with the maximum opportunity for free interchange of goods, ideas, and experiences among men. Order is the precondition of successful human living. At the international level we know that an order capable of enforcing peace is essential to survival itself. Order and freedom are not antithetical, though there will always be practical difficulties in equating them perfectly. The unity of order and freedom is essential to the growth of the real good, for this good is the growing community of personal understanding, and mutual interdependence among people. Consequently the Christian ethic always stands against artificial barriers of law or custom which segregate races or classes, and which in any way deny the right or opportunity of free and equal meeting of men in personal comradeship.

To state the political requirement in this way illustrates the difference of this approach to Christian social philosophy from the attempt to create the Good Society according to an ideal plan. So much of the actual work of state-making takes the form of ground-clearing and obstacle removing. The poll tax has to be repealed. A law forbidding discrimination in hiring or in public accommodations has to be enforced. A board of trustees has to be educated to the necessity for understanding anti-Semitism and its evils. The United Nations fights for its life. We try to find what needs to be done to save it. All this is a long way from "creating the Good Society." But this is what responsible Christian action must be. We must break up the inhuman conditions which set men against one another. We must plant such seeds as we can of a better way. But God gives the increase in ways we cannot prescribe.

Third, the political order must protect the voluntary associations of men, and the free propagation of their faith about ultimate matters. The religious group, the Church, is not the only significant voluntary group in the state, but it is the principal group whose supreme loyalty is given to something beyond the state. Karl Barth has proposed an amazingly simple principle of Christian politics. He says: "All that can be said from the standpoint of divine justification on the question (and the questions) of human law is summed up in this one statement: *'the Church must have freedom to proclaim divine justification.'* "[14] That the freedom of the Church to speak its message should be the one principle by which Christianity judges any social order may seem an absurd oversimplification. Probably it does say too little, but it is far from absurd.

Justification means making righteous. What Barth says is that where the Church is free to proclaim God's righteousness above all human righteousness; where the Church can call men to worship the God who is the judge of every state; and where the Church can publicly interpret the demand of righteousness in relation to the life about it; here we have the most fundamental of all freedoms, and the one absolute condition of the better social order. Men must be free to speak, hear, and criticize in the realm of faith. Whether such freedom can exist in a state where any church is "established" is debatable, taking human experience as a whole. We cannot say it is absolutely impossible given certain historical conditions. But Americans and many others are rightly dubious about it.[15]

Fourth, the resources of both the political order and the voluntary groups in society must be used to bring healing and mercy to broken lives. One of the truly bright strands in the dark fabric of human history is the slow but real progress of the humanitarian ideal. Lives can be reclaimed. The moral demand for humane treatment of the criminal and the sense of social responsibility for seeking his rehabilitation are precious achievements of civilization, however tragically inadequate present practice may be. There will always be those who need special care and aid from the state, the Church, or other institutions. Both in England and in America at the present time we appear ready to recognize that the good offices of courts and other public institutions may help to save many marriages which are threatened with collapse. Philanthropy which merely patches up the worst results of evil social conditions can hardly be called anything more than a necessary evil. But in the best society we can conceive men will still need to bear one another's burdens.

Fifth. Our first four principles are so widely accepted by men of good will that they sound commonplace. That does not make it less necessary to state them. We are a long way from achieving them even on the most optimistic view. The principle which we now urge is of a somewhat different character. In some measure it has been accepted in enlightened democratic society; but it always meets stubborn resistance. The fifth condition of the good society is *that every man shall be able to participate with power in the making of the decisions which affect his life; and every group shall be able to participate with power in the decisions which affect its interests as a group.* Here is the ethical frontier in the major struggles of mankind today. How shall the worker participate with power in the decisions which affect his job, his income, his security? How shall all nations, strong and weak, participate with power in the decisions in the international political order which affect their very existence and their prospects for security?

The importance of the power problem for Christian ethics derives both from the fact that power, whether economic, political, military, or spiritual, means capacity to determine life for good or ill, and from the fact that some fundamental redistribution of power is necessary as a condition of the freedom and dignity of men in their social relations. The failure to recognize the significance of power is a grave error for which traditional Christian ethics may at some points be held responsible. It has sometimes made the false assumption that where men have the spirit of love they can be indifferent to the structure of power in their social relationship. But "liberty of contract begins where equality of bargaining power exists," as Oliver Wendell Holmes said.[16] There are indeed many kinds of power, including the power of prestige, of moral conviction, of rational persuasion. That is why there can be no simple rule for calculating equality of power. But Justice Holmes points to the essential matter. If I have power over my neighbor and he has none over me, the chances are overwhelming that I will exploit him. I will probably justify my exploitation on the ground that my motives are pure. The proof of this is that in all the struggles for power in human history, those who have been powerless have been able to see the evil that is done to them; whereas those who have power both cannot and will not see the evil. To take one example: women have been systematically exploited by men in all human relations and not least in the home in all Western civilization. They have been assigned the dullest work, have been denied opportunity for self-development, have had the major decisions affecting their lives determined by men. A modern writer pleads that women might have a chance "to be something other than a nurse-maid, a scrub-woman, a delivery truck."[17] In so far as the status of women has approached equality in our society this gain cannot be attributed primarily to the moral insight of men. It was made possible through the new economic power of women which came with the technological developments in modern industry. This is but one example of the fact that the distribution of economic power is essential to the establishment of human relations on a basis of the equal dignity of all members of the community.

We have already pointed out that the existence of the power factor does not make the ethic of love irrelevant. On the contrary, love as a principle of social ethics implies that distribution and organization of power which can offer the foundation for free and constructive human relations. One of the high strategies of parental love is to allow children the growing sense of power which sets them free from either the conscious or unconscious domination of the parents. It is in such a strategy rather than in the intensity of emotional attachment that parental love reaches its highest moral plane, and comes closest to the meaning of love in its religious sense.

The word "democracy" has not appeared in our statement of the conditions of the possibility of the good society. Whether these conditions are identical with democracy is in part a matter of definition. They are not identical with all the political and ideological forms which have characterized democracy. But if basic democracy means the attempt to order the common life in such a way that these conditions are met—and I believe that basic democracy can be so defined—then the positive relationship between the Christian ethic and political and social democracy is here affirmed. All the democratic rights and freedoms are, from this Christian perspective, derived from the one natural right which belongs to every man, his right to find fulfillment in the free service and enjoyment of God and his fellows.[18]

III

The Christian hope for human society is that these conditions can be more completely fulfilled, and that within these conditions men will continue to discover and respond to the high possibilities of justice and love.

We cannot absolutely prove that these conditions can be more fully realized. Ultimate assumptions about the nature of human existence and the forces which determine it are involved. Yet some objectivity in the analysis of human possibilities is possible. We have a right to take some hope from certain facts which are being brought to light. Four recent major studies of human problems support a measure of optimism in human affairs: Arnold Toynbee's *A Study of History*; Quincy Wright's *Study of War*; Gunnar Myrdal's study of color caste in America, entitled *An American Dilemma*; and the essays edited by the cultural anthropologist, Ralph Linton, entitled *The Science of Man in the World Crisis*. These intensive analyses of the human scene by historian, social scientist, political scientist, and anthropologist, do not cover up the brutal, tragic record. If one wanted to defend Thomas Hobbes' description of human life as "nasty, brutish, and short," he could use these studies as case material. But they also reveal something more hopeful. They all reject the kind of fatalistic determinism which at times has hung like a pall over our scientific sophistication. When Mr. Toynbee says, "The more I study the record the less of a fatalist I become," he is speaking as one individual, but he expresses a judgment which is more and more finding support.[19] Neither the fatalistic pessimism of Spengler nor the mechanistic optimism of Herbert Spencer, nor yet the confident assurance of Professor Sorokin that we can chart the future on the basis of a scientific formula represent infallible truth.[20] We may believe one or the other of them. But we may also interpret the facts as supporting the belief that there are within limitations real possibilities for the exercise of human freedom in the reconstruction of the orders of existence. Myrdal says: "With all we know today, there should be the possibility to build a nation and a world where people's great propensities for sympathy and cooperation would not be so thwarted." Looking at America and the race problem he says: "America can demonstrate that justice, equality, and cooperation are possible between white and colored people."[21] Mr. Wright makes the important point that the belief in the inevitability of a great evil, such as war, will itself contribute to man's inability to deal with that evil. He concludes that the ways in which men will deal with conflict are not determined; and human intelligence and control may make possible a world order which can prevent the terrible destruction of violent warfare.[22]

To believe in human freedom is to believe that conditions do not control human decisions. Conditions make certain kinds of decisions more likely and more possible. But freedom sets the limit to all assurance that any particular human problem will be solved. The ultimate condition of the Good Society is that men shall freely will the justice and the love which are necessary to it. We need to say to ourselves cold-bloodedly that if we do not rise to the demand of our time for a wider justice and a more stable world order, there is the real possibility that what will be left of humanity will be a few crazed survivors stumbling and mumbling about in the radioactive ruins left by the atomic war. But a great demand has its own power

of calling forth a high response. What we can believe in and hope
for is the possibility of that response.[23]

3. Our hope has a third dimension. *Christian hope is sustained
by, and expressed in, faith in the Kingdom of God.* In the good
earth, and in such glimpses of the Good Society as we have we
discern a deeper reality upon which these depend. The Kingdom
of God we have said is God's love being manifested with power.
His Kingdom is present in the goodness of the earth and in the
promise of the better society. Its form in our history is that of the
reign of Christ against His enemies which are the enemies of all
human fulfillment. Beyond and yet within all political issues we
recognize the more ultimate issue of our relation to the eternal
work of God.

The Kingdom of God is disclosed among us first as judgment.
We cannot identify any earthly Good Society, even one perfected
in our imagination, with God's order. On this point structural
alterations must be made in the interpretation of the social gospel.
The minister may say: "The Kingdom of God was for Jesus something to be achieved on this earth here and now. He urged his
followers to seek to transform the whole social order until it con-
formed to the will of God and brought justice to all. . . . An
immediate task right here in our own community that will help
is to work for public power at cost."[24] But he is making a claim
which should not be made and raising hopes which should not be
raised. Public power at cost probably is one of the ways in which
the principle of distribution of economic power must be imple-
mented in modern society. But we can support that program as
Christians while refusing to claim for one political policy the
righteousness of God. This, then, should be the new imperative of
the Christian social gospel: "Let us create according to our best
wisdom, the conditions of the Good Society for the sake of the
Kingdom of God."

The Kingdom is promise and power as well as judgment. We

know our efforts are not futile. Our hope is not pinned to the success of any particular program we undertake. This belief in the continuing victory of God within the shattering of human designs is based on more than an untested faith. It is based on the continuing experience of a people who have lived by that faith, have seen it illuminated through one solitary life which is forever remembered, a people who have known a new life made possible by that memory. Here is the real Good Society in history. It is something other than political orders or ecclesiastical institutions. It is the company of imperfect folk who have seen the love of God, entrusted their lives to Him, and have begun to love one another. While we certainly do not draw the boundaries of that society at the limits of historic Christianity, and Christian theology has never done so, it is our Christian confession that such knowledge as we have of the "communion of saints" has come to us primarily through the Christian community.

Everything we have so far said about man's hope depends upon the assertion that through the transforming power of God it is possible for men to love one another. The reader who has come so far with us will already have been asking whether that assertion is made on faith, or whether it is a truth of experience. To this question we give our attention in the last chapter.

CHAPTER EIGHT

Growth in Grace: The Final Assurance

CHRISTIAN hope, we have been saying, is grounded in the structure of life. We believe we see within that structure the loving work of God. Christian hope for human society is based on the fact of God's creative and redemptive working which is woven through the whole fabric of life. One manifestation of that work is a coercive and persuasive thrust toward a human society of justice and equality. While we reject the romantic doctrine that this society gradually emerges in purity, we do believe that God wins His victories in spite of the persistent evil.

This sober hopefulness depends upon the belief that it is possible in some degree for men to love their neighbors as themselves. We must examine this belief. Is this true? Or have we been describing life as it ought to be but not as it is? Reinhold Niebuhr suggests the formula that the Christian life means a break with sin in principle but not in fact.[1] Is that where we must come out?

I

Part of the controversy over the possibility of love derives from misunderstandings of what the problem is. Some clarification is in order.

A first confusion arises if we try to prove the possibility of man's loving his neighbor simply by pointing to noble, sacrificial, and kindly behavior. Of course there is such behavior. But the question

is, What does it mean? The facts are clear. Human beings are capable of self-sacrifice. Parents gladly give their lives for their children. Men will die for their nation, and they will risk life even for someone unknown to them. The bonds of degrading habits can be broken. Alcoholics Anonymous proves this every day. Men can be converted, and can experience a new spirit which shatters old ways and releases them to live with decency and kindness. Let us add quickly that all these facts reveal something of the goodness of God and the potential goodness of man. But none of these facts answers the question which Christian faith must answer, Can a man give his life to the one real good, to the community of all things under God? Only the will to that good is the meaning of Christian love. Even the sacrifice of life for a stranger in peril may be no more than a natural response to danger or an expression of comradely feeling. Heroism both physical and moral may spring from motives quite different from the love we see in Christ.

The natural question comes: "What difference does it make what may be the source of moral qualities provided men actually achieve them?" But it makes all the difference. It makes the radical difference as to what we can hope for from human beings. Notice, if human goodness is prompted by something less than the full demand of the universal community of good, then no matter how courageous and high-minded it may be, *Somewhere this limitation will be revealed*. And that place will be just in the case where love is most needed, that is, where man must transcend his emotional attachments and instinctive responses to rise to a new level of service to the universal good. The ultimate imperative of the Gospel is, "Seek ye first the kingdom of God and his righteousness." Kierkegaard echoes the Gospel in saying, "Purity of heart is to will one thing."[2] Can man really submit even his high ideals and noble virtues to be transformed by the demands of the one final good, the Great Society of all? If so we can hope that something of that society can really grow on earth. If not, we shall still discover many great goods in human experience. But they will all finally be exposed as falling short of the actual needs of the common life. The good which could make life whole will not be ours.

The doctrine that pagan virtues are but splendid vices is relevant here, though this ancient saying is an unfortunate statement of a partial truth. There is no reason to deny that human virtues are genuine goods in God's sight as well as man's. The religious question is whether man's virtues lead him to will to serve God first and whether they support that will. Human experience gives abundant evidence that unless virtues are finally transmuted by the spirit of love they may become deadly in the service of ruthless and ignoble desires. Even kindness can make a man fail to meet the real demands of God in a given situation where something rigorous and unyielding is called for. Jacques Barzun remarks that "most of the heartburnings in the academic world come from somebody's yielding to the temptation to be kind at the wrong time."[3]

Christian love does not mean we will a good in which the self has no part. That error we have tried to refute in Chapter Three. Negation of self is a Buddhist, not a Christian, idea. But the high demand of God is to will one's own good only as it can serve and share in the good of all. To love ourselves for God's sake is the highest form of love as Bernard said.[4] It is the possibility of that love we are seeking.

A second confusion which attends the discussion of the possibility of love is related to the problem of perfectionism. Jesus said, "You must be perfect as your heavenly father is perfect."[5] The word τέλειος which is usually translated "perfect" occurs fairly frequently in Paul's letters.[6] The problem of the various forms of perfectionism in Christianity has been thoroughly analyzed in such works as Dr. Sangster's *Path to Perfection*, a study of John Wesley, and R. Newton Flews' *The Idea of Perfection in Christian Theology*.[7] The meaning of this doctrine of perfection is one problem for Christian faith. But the point to be made here is that the question of whether love is in any sense possible for man is separable from that of whether in this life he can ever perfectly love God and his neighbor. I am, for example, never quite certain whether Niebuhr means by a "break with sin in fact" a complete break. If the question is whether perfect love is possible I should certainly side with Niebuhr. But we may find it possible to assert that the beginning and maturing of the life of love is a fact. Let the possibility of perfection take its proper place as an ideal which lies always beyond existence. Or let it be the momentary glimpse of perfect love which transcends our ordinary state of being, which perhaps is what it really meant to John Wesley. But let us not insist upon the achievement of perfection in the Christian life any more than we insist upon it in the works of our hands or our minds.

With two possible sources of confusion removed we can state our thesis: It is possible for human beings, in response to the power and goodness of God, to begin to will His Kingdom above all other things and to grow toward a more mature expression of that will. In our first chapter we said that the new life is made possible through an encounter with the redemptive love of God. It involves a release from the old self and the putting on of a new. The power which works this transformation is released in the frustrated life through the discovery that the love which God demands is a love which shares our human lot and offers reconciliation. Norman Pittenger has said that what Christianity has to offer is life in God, life in charity, and life in union.[8] If that is no real offer then we have no Gospel.

Evidence is called for to support this claim. But what kind of evidence will be sufficient? We can multiply testimonies from Christian experience. We can describe Christian lives as we know them, but all of this leaves us unsatisfied. We need to probe more deeply into the kind of problem here presented for Christian thought for nothing less than the good news of Christianity is at stake.

There are three reasons why it is difficult to support any interpretation of the Christian life.

First, there is the problem presented by the kind of reality we are inquiring about, namely, human motives and the human will. Man is more than a bundle of reflexes and emotional patterns which can be studied objectively. Man is spirit. He is a free creative participant in the process of becoming. Spirit is our name for personality in action, encountering and creatively responding to the demands of life. It is man as spirit that expresses love in all the high senses of that word. It is the human will in its inward structure and intent that is the real man as Christianity sees him. The question about love is a question about spirit, motives, and personal intention.

Now, we ask, what kind of experience can enable us to pass judgment on the spirit? The answer is that all human experience is evidence. But does any experience give conclusive evidence that our interpretation is valid? In judging others we are always reduced to mediated evidence. We certainly cannot enter into another person's soul, at least never sufficiently enough to judge without question what is there.

It might appear that there is one whose spirit we can judge, that is ourself. But is a man ever really known to himself? We do not know ourselves apart from interpretation of our motives. We get the principles which we use in self-interpretation from something beyond our own experience, the categories and concepts of the group. There is a sense in which we are always seeing ourselves as others see us. Dr. E. E. Aubrey has made this point clearly in his book, *Man's Search for Himself*.[9] A vivid illustration of the problem here raised for all moral judgments is given in the experience of a lecturer who asserted to a group of Southern people that no one could practice discrimination against another race and be a Christian. To this one person replied: Suppose that your family, your school, all the groups to which you belonged and whose members you respected, practiced and justified discrimination so that you never had a chance to raise with yourself a question about it, were you then not a Christian? The lecturer was forced to make an application of the doctrine of invincible ignorance! Any claim on our thought or behavior which we have never had an opportunity to recognize cannot be held against us as free and moral beings.

Unless then we can find some kind of "intuitive" knowledge of motives which cannot be questioned, we would seem to be forever at the mercy of the historical relativities of the concepts by which groups live. One who is born, for example, into a Christian group which teaches the doctrine of perfection may be expected to interpret a decisive religious experience as the granting of perfect love by the Holy Spirit.

The fact that we misjudge our own motives is the primary difficulty of the "intuitionist" solution of the problem. Once we allow that intuitions can be faulty, we have to provide for some method and standard by which they are corrected. This takes us beyond a purely intuitional theory of knowledge. Rarely if ever does our judgment of our intentions become mature in the moment of action. It is in retrospect with the advantage of some detachment, and with the opportunity of bringing into our judgment the wider range of our knowledge that we begin to know ourselves. We often revise our estimate of the motives and interests which actually have dominated us. What we thought was profound religious stirring we may judge to have had a large mixture of adolescent romanticism. Our "devotion to the Kingdom of God" may have concealed an inward yearning for approval and power. There is clinical evidence here. The psychologist Rollo May tells of an idealistic college student who went to the Near East as a missionary only to break down when he discovered he really did not possess the spirit he was teaching. "The boys saw through our shell. The idea had got around that when we teachers talked about love, it was not Christian love for the natives at all, but love for our own ideal of love."[10]

Ours has been an age of unmasking. We have indulged in what has become almost an orgy of self-disclosure and self-abasement.

The names of Freud and Marx stand for some of the profounder discoveries about the hidden springs of conduct. Much modern literature, poetry, and painting has joined the chorus. It is difficult to sift the sense from the nonsense, but surely this whole exercise in self-analysis has yielded solid truth. We need, for example, to recognize how deeply our spiritual lives are influenced by the conditions inherent in the particular economic and social structure in which we are placed. Most people have little or no conception of how their emotional patterns and profoundest religious experiences are conditioned by the values, experiences, and frustrations which their particular role in the social order involves. To face these facts, and to be willing to follow through to the end whatever may contribute to our self-knowledge is itself an act of love, for love casts out the fear of knowing the truth about ourselves.

We now seem to be saying that we can get knowledge of our real intentions. It would be nonsense to say that we misjudge our motives unless there is some way in which misjudgments are corrected.

The solution has already been hinted at. It consists in a synthesis of intuition and critical reflection. We have to take our interpretations of human behavior as hypotheses and test them against an ever wider range of experience. That testing includes a continuing attention to whatever the special sciences tell us about the conditions and the character of human motivations. But we cannot get the truth about man simply by adding up what the sciences say. We have to gather the data of experience to achieve a coherent interpretation which includes as clear an analysis as we can make of our presuppositions about the nature of things.

Such data as we have are often like this testimony out of the concentration camps. Mme. Olga Lengyel writes:

Yet I saw many internees cling to their human dignity to the very end. The Nazis could debase them physically but they could not degrade them morally. Because of them I have not entirely lost my faith in mankind. If even in the hell of Birkenau there were those who were not necessarily inhuman to their fellow men, then there is still hope. It is that hope which keeps me alive.[11]

The facts upon which we comfortably reflect are indeed often gathered at great cost.

The work of elaborating a world view in which all our particular ideas will have their place is essential to any judgment on the nature of man. On its technical side this is the task of philosophy and theology. These disciplines can achieve a view of things which makes sense. But we cannot claim for them as much objectivity as the sciences have.[12] Psychology itself shares many of those difficulties with philosophy and theology. Professor Allport says: "Even the psychologist who honestly desires not to underestimate the complexities of personality finds himself limited by the crudity of the tools within his professional store."[13] Even with the best tools, we will always be confronted by the fact that the interpretation of human motives involves ultimate theories of the nature of things which can be tested only as they progressively illuminate more and more of the human scene. Alternative world views will always be possible. It is the fate of man to be able to know himself adequately only as he comes to know God.

One further remark about the understanding of personality which has been made possible by modern science should be made. The disclosure that the particular interests of men, whether biological, psychological, or economic, do influence not only their behavior but their self-interpretation, does not disprove the claim that love as will to the universal good is possible. We do not have to show that some pure and detached spirit of love operates in man apart from his natural interests and desires. We do not have to show that love exists completely uncorrupted by those interests. We only hold that the whole man can act with freedom, and that his act can be qualified by his will to serve the good of all things.

Any judgment on human nature runs into the problem of human

differences. There are varieties of Christian experience. We have to take into account the whole company of saints and wicked, the once-born and the twice-born, the strong of spirit and the weak, the kindly and the ruthless, those who have saved their souls by withdrawal from the world, and those who have assumed the moral risks of ecclesiastical office and public trust. Each adds something to our experience of the way of love, both in its possibility and its elusiveness. Professor Whitehead's reminder that "the intolerant use of abstractions is the major vice of the intellect" is timely for the theology of the Christian life.[14] The imposition on experience of particular patterns which define for everyone what it should be like for him to be a Christian has been a major vice not only of theology but of the Church's approach to Christian nurture.

We are not looking, then, for an indisputable judgment on what may be possible in the response of the spirit to God's demand. We are looking for a sober and responsible position which squares with as full an understanding as we can get of what the history of the Christian people reveals. The position now to be set forth is this: While it seems quite clear that perfect love is never possessed by man, the beginning of a response in love to the grace of God is possible and growth in grace as a maturing in that life is possible. In our formulation of the Christian life we have to do justice both to the grace and to the growth, for whatever progress in the life of love is possible, it is always progress within the structure of man's relationship to the creative and redemptive working of God. Growth never takes us beyond the need of grace in any of its aspects. But there can be real progress in the Christian life.

II

To break any living thing into parts, whether it be a flower or the pilgrimage of the human spirit, is to risk destroying its vital unity. Yet we must analyze, and too simple formulas for the Christian life are to be distrusted. The five principles here set forth are attempts to do justice to five aspects of the Christian life conceived as growth in response to the grace of God. These distinctions do not represent separate moments of experience. They are aspects of a total life the mystery of which lies beyond our powers of analysis. If we take any one of them in isolation from the others we fall into error.

The emphasis upon "growth" connects the New Testament conception of growth in grace with the metaphysical doctrine that the most concrete reality we know is process. Applied to the description of the Christian life, this means that our standpoint is directly opposed to that neo-orthodox doctrine which stresses the discontinuity of Christian faith with the rest of experience in such a way that it is asserted, for example, by Dr. Daniel T. Jenkins that there is "no kind of continuity between the 'old man' and the 'new man in Christ.' "[15] Our analysis presupposes that there is always continuity in human experience between any of its moments and all of its moments. The Christian life is a process in which the continuum of conditions and consequences is not escaped. Within this process God does effect a revolutionary transformation.

1. Growth in grace has a beginning. The beginning of the new life of the Christian is the birth of faith in the whole man. Faith is born out of the encounter of man with the fact of God. It is the breaking of the shell of self-centeredness and the free commitment of the self to the power and the goodness of God. Faith is more than belief though it involves belief. Faith is more than an act of will, though it involves a decision of will. Faith is response. It is the whole-souled giving of life into the keeping of God who is the absolutely trustworthy source and redeemer of life.[16]

Two points have given rise to endless controversy over the nature of faith. The first has to do with the relative significance of God's power and man's freedom in the new beginning. The second has to do with the psychological process involved, particularly the significance of emotional manifestations which may accompany conversion.

With respect to the first, there are always difficulties if we try to separate, even in thought, God's bestowal of the new life from our reception of it. It is right to emphasize that faith itself is given to us as a gift. We cannot create it by an act of will any more than we can create God's mercy for us, and bring it to ourselves by human effort. Yet God cannot bestow faith which we in our freedom will not receive. There is a double movement in faith—God toward us and we toward God. God is the initiator of all saving activity. Here it appears to me the Calvinist insistence on "predestination" is so far correct. But we need not make an artificial separation between justification by faith as the receiving of the gift of forgiveness, and regeneration as the actual beginning of the new life. There is no such separation, as Calvin himself takes great pains to make clear. If there is no element of our own freedom in our giving of ourselves to God, then the Christian life depends on a mechanical action. If we deny human freedom we make the humanist protest against religion inevitable and so far valid.

On the question of the actual psychological processes involved in the birth of faith, and particularly on the question of whether faith is given once for all, we must exercise caution. On the psychological side there is so much we do not know about religious experience. What we have said about the varieties of experience applies here. Some find faith in a dramatic experience for which they can give date and place. Some find it as an imperceptible growth, its beginning known, if at all, only in retrospect. As we shall see in a later point, we have no basis for saying that faith is always possessed once for all. Men do lose their faith. Some find it again. We can know we are telling the truth when we say this, though we should always be uncertain about judgment on any particular case. There is something in the whole person which no analysis will ever reveal.

The precise difficulty in stating the marks of true faith is illustrated by the struggle of Jonathan Edwards with this problem. For Edwards it was a pressing question. In the Great Awakening, he saw all about him—much of it produced through his own preaching—the violent psychological disturbances connected with religion. How is one to tell what is really an authentic sign of faith and what is not? Edwards' analysis is keen and uncompromising. He discusses many suggestions as to how the difference can be told, and rejects even the most plausible ones. For example, "It is no certain sign that the religious affections which persons have are such as have in them the nature of true religion, or that they have not, that they dispose persons to spend much time in religion, and to be zealously engaged in the external duties of worship."[17] Again, "It is no sign that affections are right or that they are wrong, that they make persons that have them exceedingly confident that what they experience is divine, and that they are in a good estate."[18] And Edwards avoids the error of putting faith in good works, "It is no evidence that religious affections are saving or that they are otherwise that there is an appearance of love in them."[19]

Edwards must be able to say what the distinguishing signs of faith are else he could not make these statements; but he acknowledges that he does not believe it is in God's plan to give us rules whereby "we may certainly know who of our fellow professors are his." This is God's prerogative.[20] Edwards' answer is that divine things are discerned by the spirit, hence this judgment itself is a judgment of faith. He does introduce "Christ-like ways of life," and "perseverance in the duties of the Christian." These are the best signs we have.

Edwards' treatment is a masterly blend of psychological insight and the cautious reserve appropriate in the Christian sense of the mystery of grace. But the assurance that there is a life in faith is maintained.

2. The second principle is that the life of faith is actualized in the process of life. There begins a new way of living. That the

reality of this new way was an integral part of the message of
Jesus is superbly put by Karl Holl in his comment on the distinctive
Christian notion that "God stands particularly close to the sinner."[21]
Holl points out the relation of this doctrine to Jesus' teaching:

> It is all the more astonishing that on the basis of such a conception of
> God, which seemed to dissolve all morality, Jesus nevertheless built up an
> ethic, and the most exacting ethic conceivable at that. . . . The meaning is
> clear: pardoning grace overcomes, because at the same time it encourages
> and humbles. It creates an inner affection, a feeling of gratitude which
> must find expression, and for which the highest is not too much to do. . . .
> From this follows the most splendid feature of the ethic of Jesus, namely,
> the naturalness, the spontaneous character of the action, which he sup-
> poses even in things most difficult and self-denying. . . . God takes the
> initiative: with His forgiveness He creates something quite new, out of
> which arises at once a real, close, and warm relationship to God, and with
> it at the same time a morality which ventures to take even God Himself as
> its model.[22]

The new life includes (1) a new interpretation of the meaning
of life, (2) a new devotion in the service of God, and (3) a new
participation in the working of God. These are all recognizable
processes. All involve growth in the depth, the wisdom, and the
completeness of the life of faith.

Growth in grace involves growth in the new structure of meaning
through which faith interprets life. The possession of a new meaning in itself yields power to alter life. We are interpreters. We live
in the world which is in large part shaped for us by the system of
cultural symbols and concepts which we inherit. Our very minds
and spirits are interwoven with the structure of symbols and meanings by which we interpret the world. The significance of Dr.
Hocking's remark, "What the man sees becomes the working part
of the man," has been abundantly confirmed in the psychological
clinic.[23] The process of healing the disordered personality involves
the reinterpretation of the past and the achievement of a new interpretation of the meaning of existence. The Christian revelation has

always been apprehended as the Word of God, not merely a word about life, but the entry into human history of a new meaning which has become operative in shaping the course of history.

This aspect of the new meaning in the life of faith helps us to see more deeply into the question of whether faith can ever be lost once it has become real in life. This much is true: when I have once seen my life in relation to God all further experience must be so interpreted as to include that fact. Whatever the loss of faith may mean it can never be a return simply to what life was before faith possessed it. Its meaning now is "life which has lost faith." This gives a new dimension to the bitter experience. There is a sense then in which once the life in grace has begun it can never fall completely out of its apprehension of that grace, even when we rebel against God. We have stood once within the circle of God's love. We can never move far enough to leave it entirely.

Interpretation exists within the life of devotion, for the new meaning is simply life given in service. It is the life of work in response to our vocation. Energy, intelligence, and will are enlisted in doing what needs to be done. This too is process. This working must be renewed day by day; the new life has its times of waning energy and loss of courage, its times of decision, and its times of victory in the whole-souled response to need.

The new life participates in the power of God. We do not do it all. We share in a working which is beyond our sight and our power. Our moment in time is the heir of all previous moments and of what God has accomplished in them. We are deceived by the appearance that everything is dependent upon our efforts. But the tides and powers which shape our destiny and to which we add our mite of freedom and creative decision have been running for all the ages. It follows that what we actually do is largely invisible to us. What we actually do is what our life becomes as it influences the ongoing history. We share in a destiny we can but faintly envision. We participate in a task which occupies God for eternity.

We come now to the difficult question of whether it is meaningful to speak of growth or progress in the life of love. It might appear that if we describe the Christian life as process, we should have to accept the notion of a progressive achievement. But the matter is not so simple.

3. The third principle is that there is new temptation at every stage of the Christian experience. Therefore, growth in grace is never growth away from dependence upon the continuing mercy of God.

The danger of all theories of growth in grace is that they may justify a false complacency by suggesting that achievement in the religious life puts one beyond the possibility of serious temptation and actual sin. This danger is manifest when Professor Macintosh describes the Christian experience in these terms: "Christ brings to us the salvation which consists in being indwelt and progressively delivered from the ruling power of sin. . . . As Paul might have said, the Christian life is the Christ-like life, the life of faith, hope, and unselfish love, inwardly felt and outwardly expressed."[24]

There are two reasons why this puts the matter inacceptably. The first is that the risks of freedom are not recognized. If we say the progress of the Christian life results in a freedom only to do the good then we make spiritual maturity a development out of responsibility into mechanism. There is no evidence that mature Christian experience makes new decisions automatic. Habits become established, indeed. But the meaning of every important decision is precisely that old habits do not suffice. We have the example of the prayer of Jesus prayed in agony in the garden of Gethsemane. There is every evidence that his last decision was the most difficult to make.

In the second place, there is abundant evidence that growth in the life of the spirit brings new temptations with it. The very achievements of the Christian life bring peculiar difficulties. These are not always overcome in proportion to the degree of spiritual advancement. That evidence has been gathered and powerfully presented by Reinhold Niebuhr. His analysis of the sin of moral and spiritual pride is a permanent addition to the Christian interpretation of life.[25] Sin is man's absolutizing of himself.[26] Its source lies both in man's insecurity and in his possession of something which makes a high estimate of his own wisdom and virtue plausible. The good man can always find reasons to conceive of his goodness more highly than it deserves. Behind our exaggerated estimates of our own virtue there usually lies a more or less hidden consciousness that our case is not so strong as we would have it.

A judgment confirming Niebuhr's has come from one whose orientation is somewhat different. W. E. Sangster, whose study of Wesley's doctrine of perfection we have noted, is closer to the pietist tradition, and he affirms the possibility of love more unequivocally than does Niebuhr. Yet Sangster concludes that the claim to perfection has been a mistake. It is part of the strategy of the Christian life to recognize the saints' capacity for self-deception.

John Calvin was surely right when he said that humility is the first, second, and third truth about the Christian life, and most contemporary theology agrees.[27] The claim to any complete possession of Christian love reveals a superficial knowledge of how deep sin is and how frail we are. "However much thou progress thou must set thy hope on mercy," says St. Augustine.[28]

Our first three principles affirm growth in the Christian life; yet we have now said this growth never gives us such firm spiritual achievement that we can say our goodness is adequate. We need to go on then to the statement of the fourth principle.

4. Real growth in the strength to love and serve God is possible. Growth in grace means that there can be progress in the expression of Christian wisdom and love. There is no contradiction between this and the third principle for we do not say that such growth puts man beyond the possibility of temptation and the subtle corruptions of the spirit. We say only that there can be growth in the

discernment of what it is that corrupts and in the power to meet temptation.

The term "progress" very likely confuses the issue here for some. In our modern usage it connotes a smooth and all but inevitable movement toward a goal. But no reader of Bunyan's *Pilgrim's Progress* need fall into this illusion. Bunyan's description of the Christian journey through life is one of the most realistic ever produced. There are giants to be fought at nearly every turn in the road, and the Pilgrim trembles to see at the very gate of heaven a byway to the pit. But there are experiences of victory, and a vision of the gates of glory at the end. Calvin's description of the Christian life comes from another ruggedly realistic mind. He faces all the difficulties but finally leaves this door of hope open. "No man will be so unhappy but that he may every day make some progress, however small."[29]

Growth in grace may be best interpreted as progress toward spiritual maturity. Dr. Moffatt usually translates the New Testament word τέλειος as "mature." Maturity in the life of loving service is a recognizable fact in Christian experience.

Christian maturity means progress in self-understanding which is one of the prerequisites of works of love. We correctly speak of progress toward a fuller awareness of the meaning of love and of the nature of sin. There has been, for example, a growth in grace in this respect in the modern Church's understanding of social sin. The recognition that love must bear the burdens of the common life, that what appears as personal holiness may mask an irresponsible attitude toward social injustice, and that the task of love includes social reconstruction marks an advance in Christian maturity. And we know that all growth toward maturity is sustained by personal relationships. It is false to assume that grace works only in the individual.

Maturity in the life of love means increasing skill in meeting the obligations which love lays upon us. Every minister knows people of good will in his parish upon whom he relies because they know, often better than he does, what needs to be done for the person in need. The minister knows of others, not lacking in good will, who are inept in situations which demand special sensitivity and insight. Christian maturity involves the development of the skills and intelligence through which love can do its work. It is here that much of the responsibility of Christian education lies. We have to speak cautiously about increasing the skills of the spiritual life. It is God's work more than ours. We can, however, try to provide the conditions under which love has a chance to grow, and do its work well. A. D. Lindsay has wisely observed:

> The difference between ordinary people and saints is not that saints fulfill the plain duties which ordinary men neglect. The things saints do have not usually occurred to ordinary people at all. . . . "Gracious" conduct is somehow like the work of an artist. It needs imagination and spontaneity. It is not a choice between presented alternatives but the creation of something new.[30]

It may be objected that we are speaking here not of growth in love but in skill and insight. I reply that these cannot be absolutely separated. Love itself is necessary to growth in knowledge of other persons. Growth of insight may lead to a deeper appreciation and self-giving. Love which has capacity for social imagination, and for a skillful dealing with human problems, is strengthened in itself. Growth in grace is growth in a wise, continually renewed appreciation of the things which serve and the things which destroy, and the mastery of ways of dealing with both.

Christian maturity involves, then, progress in our capacity to love. This is the most difficult principle to affirm. Let us quickly observe that if Christian experience means anything at all it is also the most difficult to deny. Surely the New Testament affirms it: "Work out your own salvation with fear and trembling for it is God who worketh in you."[31] "The Lord make you to increase and abound in love one toward another, and toward all men."[32] "Seeing that ye have put off the old man with his doings and have put on the new man that is being renewed unto knowledge after the image of him that created him."[33] The difference between the beginning of life in love and whatever fuller realization of love comes to be may be slight indeed. But there can be no Christian life at all unless there is some real meaning in progress in strength to express love. If that be not true then the meaning of life is realized only in moments of vision which do not affect our earthly existence except by relating us to something outside of it. The New Testament, the message of Jesus, the existence of the Church become inexplicable. Sangster rightly opposes the tendency in contemporary theology to stress the impossibility of holiness. It is as dangerous an error as that involved in too simple doctrines of sanctification. We need the balance of the Westminster Confession which rings with a new clarity and power at the close of our inquiry into the secret of the Christian life. The Confession allows no extravagant self-appraisal. It requires a searching and reverent humility before the righteousness of Christ. But it does not shut the door to our growth in such love as God in Christ has made possible for us:

> When God converts a sinner, and translates him into the state of grace, he freeth him from his natural bondage under sin, and by his grace alone enables him freely to will and to do that which is spiritually good; yet so, as that by reason of his remaining corruption, he doth not perfectly nor only will that which is good, but doth also will that which is evil. The will of man is made perfectly and immutably free to good alone in the state of Glory only.[34]

5. The fifth principle brings into view a new dimension of our human pilgrimage toward the light. There is the last question of the Christian's relation to the things loved in this life, and the nature of his hope in the face of death. Growth in grace involves maturity in the kind of attachment we have to the goods of this earthly existence. The principle may be stated thus: Growth in Christian maturity is growth in love for all the goods of mortal life, and at the same time it is growth in the capacity for detachment

of our ultimate faith and hope from dependence upon our particular plans and interests. Christian detachment is not a denial of the ultimate worth of created things; but it is a willingness to yield all things to the transformation of the passage of time and to surrender them to the ultimate order of God's Kingdom. Even the fate of conscious personality we entrust in death to God's keeping without knowing exactly how His care for us will be expressed.

Our discussion in this book has centered on the problem of hope. That hope has many dimensions in Christian experience. There is a legitimate hope for good in every human situation. We have said that hope that one's own spirit might grow in love to God and man is not vain, for God's grace is real. Yet in every particular human hope there is a link to a victory which transcends earthly fortune and misfortune. The wisdom of life lies in the discovery that joy belongs only to him who can submit all his own hopes to the cause of the great community of good which life on earth can never fully define or capture.

Paul's faith that "love hopeth all things" is not sentimentality. It is the affirmation which Christian faith must make about what it means to trust in God. Only the man whose hope can stand the defeat of any particular project is free to hope "for all things," that is, for whatever good may really be possible under God. Such a faith is not flight from the responsibilities of this life. The God we serve is the giver of this life with its obligations and possibilities. There is no situation in which the Christian cannot find meaning and hope. There is no social wrong which need remain unattacked, unmitigated, unreformed. There is no private desperate struggle with anxiety and bitterness and failure which cannot yield new hope when we discover that God does not leave us forsaken. But those who know this, while they are released to spend themselves in doing what needs to be done, live with a certain divine carelessness concerning earthly fortunes. Their hope sees beyond the years and they live in this demanding present under the everlasting assurance of God's love.

NOTES

CHAPTER ONE *Two Theories of Man's Destiny*

1) F. D. Roosevelt, Fourth Inaugural Address, January 20, 1945. President Harry S. Truman in his Navy Day address in New York City, October 27, 1945, said, "We know that we cannot attain perfection in this world overnight. We shall not let our search for perfection obstruct our steady progress toward international co-operation."

2) Milton, *Paradise Lost,* Bk. XI, p. 360 (New York: Modern Library ed., 1942).

3) Jonathan Edwards, *A History of the Work of Redemption, Works* (Leavitt and Allen reprint of the Worcester ed., New York, 1843), Vol. I, p. 510.

4) Reinhold Niebuhr, *The Nature and Destiny of Man* (New York: Charles Scribner's Sons, 1941-43), Vol. II, pp. 16-34.

5) Characteristic liberal works are Walter Rauschenbusch, *A Theology for the Social Gospel* (New York: The Macmillan Compay, 1917); Eugene W. Lyman, *The Meaning and Truth of Religion* (New York: Charles Scribner's Sons, 1933); and Robert L. Calhoun, *God and the Common Life* (New York: Charles Scribner's Sons, 1935). It is to be noted that later writings of the last two represent theological developments in the same direction suggested in this book, as does also John Bennett, *Christian Realism* (New York: Charles Scribner's Sons 1941). The Ritschlian theology, both in its original statement and in its American development, presents a special problem in relation to what I have characterized as "liberalism," but the discussion of Ritschlian movement deserves a full treatment in itself. Of course, "liberal Christianity" is not exclusively Protestant. See Don Luigi Sturzo, "The Catholic Church and Christian Democracy," *Social Action,* Vol. X, No. 5, May 15, 1944; also Edward R. Hardie, Jr., "Liberalism and Catholic Thought in England 1860-1940," in *Liberal Theology: an Appraisal,* ed. David E. Roberts and Henry P. Van Dusen (New York: Charles Scribner's Sons, 1942).

For historical and critical accounts of liberal theology in America see Richard Niebuhr, *The Kingdom of God in America* (New York: Harper & Brothers, 1937), chap. iv; Heinrich Frick, *Das Reich Gottes in amerikanischer und in deutscher Theologie der Gegenwart* (Giessen, 1926); W. A. Visser 't Hooft, *The Background of the Social Gospel in America* (Haarlem, 1928), chaps. ii, vii; D. D. Williams, *The Andover Liberals* (New York: King's Crown Press, 1941); C. H. Hopkins, *The Rise of the Social Gospel in American Protestantism 1865-1915* (New Haven: Yale University Press, 1940).

6) Hymn by Ozora S. Davis, "At Length There Dawns the Glorious Day,"

written in 1909. From *Praise and Service,* ed. H. Augustine Smith (New York: Appleton-Century-Crofts, 1932).

7) W. Rauschenbusch, *op. cit.,* p. 141.

8) Cf. G. Lowes Dickinson, *Is Immortality Desirable?* (Boston: Houghton Mifflin Company, 1909).

9) Harry Emerson Fosdick, *Christianity and Progress* (New York: Fleming H. Revell Company, 1922), p. 178.

10) Hanson W. Baldwin in The New York *Times,* February 7, 1945.

11) Typical expressions of the general viewpoint of neo-orthodox theology will be found in Karl Barth, *The Knowledge of God and the Service of God According to the Teaching of the Reformation* (New York: Charles Scribner's Sons, 1939), his *Credo,* English trans. (New York: Charles Scribner's Sons, 1936), and Emil Brunner, *Man in Revolt* (Philadelphia: Westminster Press, 1947). W. W. Bryden, *The Christian's Knowledge of God* (Toronto: Thomas Nelson & Sons Ltd., 1940), is an able statement of the issues neo-orthodoxy raises with liberalism. Two less technical works by American representatives of the school are John A. Mackay, *A Preface to Christian Theology* (New York: The Macmillan Company, 1941), and Edwin Lewis, *The Faith We Declare* (Nashville: Abingdon-Cokesbury Press, 1939). Reinhold Niebuhr's major work is the Gifford Lectures, *The Nature and Destiny of Man,* 2 vols.

12) On Niebuhr's view of myth see "The Truth in Myths" in *The Nature of Religious Experience,* ed. J. S. Bixler (New York: Harper & Brothers, 1937). The analysis of sin is found in *The Nature and Destiny of Man,* Vol. I, chaps. vii-ix.

13) Niebuhr insists he takes a more positive and constructive view of the possibilities of social action and reconstruction than do the Continental Barthians, and this may be the case. But on the question of the relation of the love of God to the possibilities of history I can see little difference in his Gifford Lectures from Emil Brunner's *The Divine Imperative* (Philadelphia: The Westminster Press, 1947).

14) Karl Barth, *Church and State* (London: S.C.M. Press, 1939), p. 55.

15) Quoted in John Baillie, *What Is Christian Civilization?* (New York: Charles Scribner's Sons, 1945), p. 33.

16) Recalling the phrase in Clifford Bax's hymn, "Turn Back O Man."

17) Reinhold Niebuhr, "Ten Years That Shook My World," *The Christian Century,* Vol. 56, No. 1, April 26, 1939, p. 544.

18) Reinhold Niebuhr, "Faith to Live By," *The Nation,* Vol. 164, February 22, 1947, pp. 205-9.

19) Romans 8:22-24.

20) I Thessalonians 3:12-13. Moffatt translation.

21) S. J. Case, *The Christian Philosophy of History* (Chicago: University of Chicago Press, 1943), p. 213.

22) A. C. Garnett, *A Realistic Philosophy of Religion* (New York: Harper & Brothers, 1942), p. 176.

23) F. Ernest Johnson, *The Social Gospel Re-examined* (New York: Harper & Brothers, 1940).

24) This judgment is based upon Karl Barth, *The Christian Life* (London: S.C.M. Press, 1930), and *The Knowledge of God and the Service of God According to the Teaching of the Reformation,* esp. Lectures XI-XIII. Later writings of Barth have been surprisingly "activistic." Judgment as to whether Barth's theology adequately interprets the moral demand in the Christian life must await the completion of his *Church Dogmatics.*

25) Reinhold Niebuhr, *The Nature and Destiny of Man,* Vol. II, *passim.* There are many qualifications and apparently contradictory statements in Niebuhr's treatment of the Christian life. He says that in Christian experience "the individual is actually freed to live a life of serenity and creativity" (p. 58), and again, "there is no limit to either sanctification in individual life or social perfection in collective life . . . except that there will be some corruption . . . on the new level of achievement" (p. 156). If this is the position I should agree with it; but both statements involve a break with sin in fact as well as in principle.

The criticism I offer of Niebuhr's formulation is concurred in by Robert L. Calhoun's reviews of the Gifford Lectures, *Journal of Religion,* Vol. 21, No. 4, 1941, pp. 473 ff., and Vol. 24, No. 1, 1944, pp. 59 ff., and by Wilhelm Pauck, "Luther and the Reformation," *Theology Today,* Vol. III 1946-47, esp. pp. 323 ff.

26) *Ibid.,* p. 125.

27) *Ibid.,* p. 189.

28) Emil Brunner, *Man in Revolt,* p. 489.

CHAPTER TWO   *God: The Creator and Redeemer*

1) I have tried to support this statement in "Brunner and Barth on Philosophy," *The Journal of Religion,* Vol. XXVII, No. 4, October, 1947.

2) This saying is cited and discussed in the paper just noted.

3) Emil Brunner, *Man in Revolt,* p. 91.

4) Dorothy M. Emmet, *The Nature of Metaphysical Thinking* (London: Macmillan & Co., 1946), pp. 208-11.

5) Charles Hartshorne, *Beyond Humanism* (New York: Harper & Brothers, 1937), p. 6.

6) Cf. A. N. Whitehead, *Process and Reality* (New York: The Macmillan Company, 1936). "The functioning of one actual entity in the self-recreation of another actual entity is the 'objectification' of the former for the latter actual entity," p. 38.

7) Charles Hartshorne, *Man's Vision of God* (New York: Harper & Brothers, 1941). While I do not share Professor Hartshorne's idealistic theory of knowledge my indebtedness to his analysis of the idea of God is great.

8) A. C. Garnett, *op. cit.* Cf. his *God in Us* (New York: Harper & Brothers, 1945).

9) John Baillie, *Our Knowledge of God* (New York: Charles Scribner's Sons, 1939), p. 178.

10) A. N. Whitehead, *Science and the Modern World* (New York: The Macmillan Company, 1931), p. 275.

11) Acts 14:17.

12) I have dealt somewhat more fully with the methodological problem in "Theology and Truth," *The Journal of Religion*, Vol. XXII, No. 4, October, 1942, and "Truth in the Theological Perspective," *The Journal of Religion*, Vol. XXVIII, No. 4, October, 1948.

13) Cf. William E. Hocking's comment on Whitehead's organismic metaphysics, *Science and the Idea of God* (Chapel Hill: University of North Carolina Press, 1944), pp. 108-9. Cf. Robert L. Calhoun, *op. cit.*, p. 159.

14) Agreeing with both Hocking and Whitehead as to the significance of ideal possibilities in determining process, cf. William E. Hocking, *Science and the Idea of God*, p. 110.

15) Wordsworth, *The Prelude*, Bk. I, lines 341-44.

16) Lillian Smith, from a letter published in *War and Post-War*, issued by Louis Adamic, Vol. III, Nos. 9-10, September-October, 1944, p. 1.

17) Cf. John Bennett's analysis of the problem in *Christian Realism*, Appendix.

18) Edwin Markham, "Victory in Defeat," from *The Shoes of Happiness and Other Poems* (New York: Random House, 1945), p. 347. Reprinted by permission of Mr. Virgil Markham.

19) See Nels F. S. Ferré, *Evil and the Christian Faith* (New York: Harper & Brothers, 1947).

20) A. Ritschl, *The Christian Doctrine of Justification and Reconciliation* 3rd ed. (New York: Charles Scribner's Sons, 1900), chap. viii. For criticism of the Ritschlian interpretation of forgiveness see Paul Lehmann, *Forgiveness* (New York: Harper & Brothers, 1940).

21) Josiah Royce, *The Problem of Christianity* (New York: The Macmillan Company, 1914). See especially Lecture VI, Vol. I.

22) F. Ernest Johnson, *op. cit.*, p. 85.

23) Lewis Mumford, *The Condition of Man* (New York: Harcourt, Brace and Company, 1944), p. 148.

24) II Corinthians 5:17. Cf. Galatians 6:15.

25) Romans 8:24.

26) Eugene W. Lyman, *op. cit.*, p. 12.

27) Francis H. Stead, *The Story of Social Christianity* (New York: George H. Doran, 1924), 2 Vols.

28) James Moffatt, *Grace in the New Testament* (New York: Harper & Brothers, 1932), p. 21.

29) H. R. Mackintosh's summary of Paul's doctrine. "Grace" in James Hastings, *Encyclopedia of Religion and Ethics* (New York: Charles Scribner's Sons, 1910).

30) *Edinburgh Conference on Faith and Order,* chap. ii, p. 1.

31) W. H. Auden, "In Time of War," *The Collected Poetry of W. H. Auden* (New York: Random House, 1945), p. 347. Reprinted by permission of Random House.

CHAPTER THREE *Man's Real Good*

1) Amos N. Wilder, *The Spiritual Aspects of the New Poetry* (New York: Harper & Brothers, 1940), p. 164.

2) Luke 17:21; John 18:36.

3) Mark 8:35.

4) John 5:24.

5) I John 4:8.

6) Richard Niebuhr's characterization of the Christian view of man in *The Kingdom of God in America,* p. 102.

7) Anders Nygren, *Agape and Eros* (London: S.P.C.K., English trans., Pt. I, 1932, Pt. II, 1938).

8) *Ibid.,* Part I, p. 174.

9) *Ibid.,* p. 95.

10) *Ibid.,* p. 51.

11) *Ibid.,* p. 68.

12) *Ibid.,* Pt. II, p. 406.

13) *Ibid.,* Pt. II, p. 128.

14) *Ibid.,* Pt. II, pp. 426 ff.

15) *Ibid.,* Pt. II, pp. 516-17.

16) Reinhold Niebuhr, *The Nature and Destiny of Man,* Vol. II, p. 68-9.

17) *Ibid.,* Vol. II, p. 76.

18) *Ibid.,* Vol. II, p. 69.

19) *Ibid.,* Vol. II, p. 72.

20) *Ibid.,* Vol. II, p. 95.

21) *Ibid.,* Vol. II, p. 90.

22) *Ibid.,* Vol. II, p. 88. Niebuhr has recently written that the term "self-love" should be dropped from the discussion because "it is too inexact." He continues, "The Christian criticism of self-love is primarily directed against the self's preoccupation with itself by which preoccupation it narrows and impoverishes its life." *Christianity and Society,* Spring, 1948, p. 27.

But this statement would seem to come all the way to a definition of love as the will to complete mutuality.

23) St. Augustine, *On the Freedom of the Will*, chap. xvii, paragraphs 45, 46.

24) My indebtedness here is to H. N. Wieman and Charles Hartshorne, and to Dr. Harold Bosley's analysis in *The Quest for Religious Certainty* (New York: Harper & Brothers, 1939).

25) Willard L. Sperry, *The Disciplines of Liberty* (New Haven: Yale University Press, 1921), p. 175.

26) Kahlil Gibran, *The Prophet* (New York: Alfred A. Knopf, 1934), p. 39.

27) N. Berdyaev, *The Destiny of Man* (New York: Charles Scribner's Sons, 1937), pp. 167-68.

28) Robert L. Calhoun, "The Dilemma of Humanitarian Modernism," in the Oxford Conference volume, *The Christian Understanding of Man*, ed. J. H. Oldham (New York: Harper & Brothers, 1938), p. 81.

CHAPTER FOUR   *The Kingdom of God and the Kingdoms of This World*

1) E. B. White, *The Wild Flag* (Boston: Houghton Mifflin Company, 1946), pp. 144-48.

2) E. H. Carr, *The Twenty Years' Crisis* (London: Macmillan & Company, 1942), chap. iv.

3) Attributed to Bismarck.

4) Erich Frank, *Philosophical Understanding and Religious Truth* (New York: Oxford University Press, 1945), p. 128.

5) Jacob Burckhardt, *Force and Freedom*, ed. J. H. Nichols (New York: Pantheon Books, Inc., 1943), p. 115.

6) Hans J. Morgenthau, "The Evil of Politics and the Ethics of Evil," *Ethics*, Vol. LVI, No. 1, October, 1945, p. 14.

7) *Ibid.*, p. 17.

8) E. H. Carr, *op. cit.*, p. 279.

9) Genesis 1.

10) Reinhold Niebuhr, *The Nature and Destiny of Man*, Vol. II, p. 22.

11) *Ibid.*, Vol. I, pp. 262-63.

12) Reinhold Niebuhr, *Christianity and Power Politics* (New York: Charles Scribner's Sons, 1940), p. 92. Cf. *Nature and Destiny of Man* II, p. 82.

13) William E. Hocking, *Man and the State* (New Haven: Yale University Press, 1926), p. 101.

14) See Francis J. McConnell, *Christianity and Coercion* (Nashville: Abingdon-Cokesbury Press, 1933), pp. 72, 107-8.

15) Frank Knight, *Freedom and Reform* (New York: Harper & Brothers, 1947), pp. 390 ff.

16) T. V. Smith, *The Legislative Way of Life* (Chicago: University of Chicago Press, 1940), pp. 15-16.

17) Quoted in Horace Cayton and St. Clair Drake, *Black Metropolis* (New York: Harcourt, Brace and Company, 1945), p. 362.

18) T. V. Smith, *The Democratic Tradition in America* (New York: Farrar & Rinehart, Inc., 1941), p. 48.

19) William E. Hocking, *Man and the State*, p. 10.

20) Cf. H. W. Laidler, *Social-Economic Movements* (New York: Thomas Y. Crowell Company, 1945), pp. 640-48.

21) G. W. F. Hegel, *Philosophy of Religion* (London: Kegan Paul, 1895), Vol. II, p. 83.

22) See Sumner H. Schlicter, *The Challenge of Industrial Organization* (Ithaca: Cornell University Press, 1947) for a judicious analysis.

23) C. S. Golden and H. Ruttenberg, *The Dynamics of Industrial Democracy* (New York: Harper & Brothers, 1942).

24) Reinhold Niebuhr, *The Nature and Destiny of Man*, Vol. I., p. 278.

25) Dr. George Buttrick's phrase; *Prayer* (Nashville: Abingdon-Cokesbury Press, 1942), p. 118.

26) Reinhold Niebuhr, *The Nature and Destiny of Man*, Vol. II., p. 72.

27) Emil Brunner, *The Divine Imperative*, p. 445.

28) *Ibid.*, p. 224.

29) Emil Brunner, *Justice and the Social Order* (New York: Harper & Brothers, 1945), p. 128. Cf. his *Revelation and Reason* (Philadelphia: Westminster Press, 1946), chap. xxi.

30) Martin Buber, *I and Thou*, trans. R. G. Smith (Edinburgh: T. & T. Clark, 1937).

31) *The Talmudic Anthology*, ed. Lewis I. Newman (New York: Behrman House, Inc., 1945), p. 179.

32) Martin Luther, *Secular Authority, To What Extent It Should Be Obeyed?* (Philadelphia: A. J. Holman, 1930), Vol. VI, p. 265.

33) Cf. Karl Jaspers, *Man in the Modern Age*, trans. Eden and Cedar Paul (New York: Henry Holt and Company, Inc., 1933).

34) Emil Brunner, *The Divine Imperative*, p. 326.

35) *Ibid.*, p. 327.

36) *Ibid.*, p. 85.

37) *Ibid.*, p. 73.

38) *Ibid.*, p. 223.

39) *Ibid.*, p. 222.

40) A. N. Whitehead, *Process and Reality*, p. 164.

41) Jacques Barzun, *Teacher in America* (Boston: Little, Brown & Company, 1945), p. 191.

42) Annual Report of the New York State Commission Against Discrimination, New York State Executive Department, 1946.

43) T. V. Smith, *op. cit.*, p. 71.

44) Carey McWilliams in *Now*, a semi-monthly journal, February and March, 1946.

45) *Ibid.*

46) Emil Brunner, *The Divine Imperative*, p. 457.

47) Reported in *The Christian Century*, Vol. 61, March 1, 1944, p. 260.

48) R. M. MacIver, *The Web of Government* (New York: The Macmillan Company, 1947), p. 194.

49) Quoted in W. E. Hocking, *Man and the State*, pp. 264-65.

CHAPTER FIVE   *Time, Progress, and the Kingdom of God*

1) A. N. Whitehead, *Process and Reality*.

2) N. Berdyaev, *op. cit.*, pp. 317 ff.

3) Cf. Joseph Haroutunian, *Wisdom and Folly in Religion* (New York: Charles Scribner's Sons, 1940), pp. 35-36.

4) Reinhold Niebuhr, *The Nature and Destiny of Man*, Vol. II, *passim*.

5) Paul Tillich, in the Oxford Conference volume, *The Kingdom of God and History*, ed. J. H. Oldham (Chicago: Willett, Clark & Company, 1938), pp. 113-14.

6) S. J. Case, *op cit.*, p. vi.

7) *Ibid.*, pp. 213-15.

8) *Ibid.*, p. 218.

9) *Ibid.*, p. 211.

10) A. N. Whitehead, *Adventures of Ideas* (New York: The Macmillan Company, 1933), pp. 30-31.

11) *Ibid.*, p. 205.

12) A. N. Whitehead, *Process and Reality*, p. 160.

13) *Ibid.*, "We are therefore left with the final opposites joy and sorrow, good and evil . . ." (p. 518). "Thus the universe is to be conceived as attaining the active self-expression of its own variety of opposites" (p. 531).

14) For a development of this theme of Whitehead's see B. E. Meland, *Seeds of Redemption* (New York: The Macmillan Company, 1947).

15) John Macmurray, *The Clue to History* (New York: Harper & Brothers, 1939), p. 237.

16) *Ibid.*, p. 220.

17) *Ibid.*, p. xi.

18) *Ibid.*, p. 206.

19) A. N. Whitehead, *Process and Reality*, pp. 126, 533.

20) Max Otto, *The Human Enterprise* (New York: Appleton-Century-Crofts, 1940), p. 369; cf. his *Natural Laws and Human Hopes* (New York: Henry Holt and Company, 1926).

21) George Gamow, *The Birth and Death of the Sun* (New York: Penguin Books, 1945), pp. 104-5, 154.

22) Winfred E. Garrison, "Reflections on the Goal of History," *The Christian Century*, Vol. 55, No. 2, 1938, p. 959.

23) This truth has been most clearly expressed in Charles Hartshorne, *Man's Vision of God*.

24) John Bennett, *op cit.*, Appendix.

25) This confusion seems to me patent in W. H. Sheldon, *America's Progressive Philosophy* (New Haven: Yale University Press, 1942).

26) N. Berdyaev, *Slavery and Freedom* (New York: Charles Scribner's Sons, 1944), pp. 257, 260-61.

27) For incisive criticism see Reinhold Niebuhr, *The Nature and Destiny of Man*, Vol. I, pp. 116-18.

28) S. Kierkegaard, *Philosophical Fragments* (Princeton: Princeton University Press, 1942), pp. 44 ff.

29) S. Kierkegaard, *Repetition* (Princeton: Princeton University Press, 1941). Quotation from Kierkegaard's papers of notes intended to explain the meaning of "repetition," p. 29.

30) S. Kierkegaard, *Philosophical Fragments*, p. 64.

31) *Ibid.*, p. 41.

32) *Ibid.*, p. 15.

33) S. Kierkegaard, *Repetition*, p. 34.

34) S. Kierkegaard, *Training in Christianity* (New York: Oxford University Press, 1941), p. 57.

35) *Ibid.*, p. 216.

36) S. Kierkegaard, *Philosophical Fragments*, p. 14.

37) S. Kierkegaard, *The Point of View*, trans. W. Lowrie (New York: Oxford University Press, 1939), p. 81.

38) S. Kierkegaard, *The Attack upon "Christendom"* (Princeton: Princeton University Press, 1944), p. 44.

39) S. Kierkegaard, *Training in Christianity*, p. 65.

40) *Ibid.*, p. 109.

41) *Ibid.*, pp. 205 ff.

42) S. Kierkegaard, *Philosophical Fragments*, p. 91.

43) *Ibid.*, p. 62.

44) Paul S. Minear, "Time and the Kingdom," *The Journal of Religion*, Vol. XXIV, No. 2., April, 1944, p. 85. Cf. his *Eyes of Faith* (Philadelphia: Westminster Press, 1946), Oscar Cullmann, *Christus und die Zeit* (Zurich: 1946), and Karl Barth, *Credo*. For analysis of contemporary literature on the eschatological problem see Amos Wilder, "The Eschatology of the Gospels in Recent Discussion," *Journal of Religion*, Vol. XXVIII, No. 3, July, 1948.

45) *Ibid.*, p. 81.

46) *Ibid.*, p. 83.

47) I John 3:2; Romans 13:12.

48) Charles Hartshorne, *Man's Vision of God*, pp. 227-28.

49) I Corinthians 15:25-26.

50) Colossians 2:15.

51) John Knox, *Christ the Lord* (New York: Harper & Brothers, 1945), p. 123. Cf. W. A. Visser 't Hooft, *The Kingship of Christ* (New York: Harper & Brothers, 1948).

52) John 1:1.

53) Visser 't Hooft, *The Kingship of Christ*, p. 17.

54) See a comment on Barth's interpretation of the war in a letter by E. G. Homrighausen in *The Christian Century*, Vol. 56, No. 21, May 24, 1939, p. 678.

55) I Corinthians 13:12.

56) II Corinthians 4:8-12.

CHAPTER SIX *The Divine Call and Man's Response*

1) Lincoln Steffens, *Autobiography* (New York: Harcourt, Brace and Company, Inc., 1931), p. 611.

2) T. V. Smith, *op. cit.*, p. 87.

3) F. J. E. Woodbridge, *The Son of Apollo* (Boston: Houghton Mifflin Company, 1929), p. 82.

4) Phillips Brooks, "The Christ," *Addresses* (Boston: Chas. E. Brown, 1893), p. 135.

5) Willard L. Sperry, "Our Moral Chaos," *Fortune*, Vol. XXV, No. 5, May, 1942, p. 108.

6) Arthur E. Holt, *This Nation Under God* (New York: Harper & Brothers, 1939), pp. 46-54, 109.

7) The official position of the Roman Church on political orders is that the Church can adapt itself to various types of government, whether monarchic or republican, aristocratic or democratic. See the encyclical *Dilectissima Nobis*, June 3, 1933, paragraph 6. For the struggle for democratic ideas in the Church see Don Luigi Sturzo, "The Catholic Church and Christian Democracy," *Social Action*, May 15, 1944. Cf. Jacques Maritain, *Christianisme et Democratie* (New York: La Maison Francaise, 1943).

8) Anton Koch, *A Handbook of Moral Theology*, ed. Arthur Preuss (St. Louis: B. Herder Book Company, 1925), Vol. I, p. 7.

9) Cf. J. S. Whale, *Christian Doctrine* (New York: The Macmillan Company, 1941), pp. 144-49.

10) Anton Koch, *op. cit.*, Vol. V, p. 500.

11) Cf. Reinhold Niebuhr, *The Nature and Destiny of Man*, Vol. I, p. 221. "The whole imposing structure of Thomist ethics is in one of its aspects, no more than a religious sanctification of the relativities of the feudal social system as it flowered in the thirteenth century."

12) For the Catholic teaching see the encyclical of Pius XI, *Casti Connubi*, December, 1930. Analysis and commentary by the Rev. Edgar Schmiedeler, *Christian Marriage* (Huntington, Indiana: Our Sunday Visitor Press, 1938). Cf. Edward R. Moore, *The Case against Birth Control* (New York: Appleton-Century-Crofts, 1931). For a Protestant statement in nontheological terms see Katherine Salter, "Answer to a Catholic Mother," *Protestant*, Vol. 5, No. 6, March, 1944, pp. 41 ff.

13) Cf. G. G. Coulton, *Five Centuries of Religion*, 3 vols. (New York: The Macmillan Company, 1923-36).

14) Anton Koch, *op. cit.*, Vol. V, p. 136.

15) *The Christian News Letter*, No. 75, April 2, 1941.

16) Karl Holl, "Die Geschichte des Wortes Beruf," *Gesammelte Aufsätze zur Kirchengeschichte* (1928), Vol. III, and his study of Luther's views of the calling in Vol. I, esp. pp. 239-87.

17) Max Weber, *The Protestant Ethic and the Spirit of Capitalism*, trans. Talcott Parsons (New York: Charles Scribner's Sons, 1930). R. H. Tawney, *Religion and the Rise of Capitalism* (New York: Harcourt, Brace and Company, Inc., 1926).

18) Robert L. Calhoun, *God and the Common Life;* Emil Brunner, *The Divine Imperative,* have already been noted.

19) Robert L. Calhoun, *God and the Common Life*, p. 71.

20) *Ibid.*, p. 71.

21) *Ibid.*, p. 225.

22) Cf. Robert L. Calhoun, "The Dilemma of Humanitarian Modernism," in the Oxford Conference volume, *The Christian Understanding of Man,* esp. pp. 75 ff.

23) Emil Brunner, *The Divine Imperative*, p. 206.

24) Chap. IV, *supra.*

25) Emil Brunner, *The Divine Imperative*, p. 203.

26) I am indebted to Dr. James Luther Adams for pointing this out. There are emphases in Brunner's book which go in a different direction from this on the rigidity of the orders; but the view of the world as *process* is never adequately realized.

27) I Corinthians 7:20; Ephesians 1:18.

28) Allen Haden, "Latin America," in Quincy Wright, *A Foreign Policy for the United States* (Chicago: University of Chicago Press, 1947), p. 227.

29) William Temple, *Christianity and Social Order* (New York: Penguin Books, 1942), p. 78.

30) Micah 6:8; Jeremiah 31:33.

31) Luke 10:27.

32) I Corinthians 6:12. Cf. Paul Ramsey, "A Theology of Social Action," *Social Action*, October 15, 1946, p. 29.

33) St. Augustine, *In Epist. Joannis ad Parthos*, Tr. vii, 8.

34) I. Kant, *The Fundamental Principles of the Metaphysic of Ethics,* trans. Otto Manthey-Zorn (New York: Appleton-Century-Crofts, 1938), p. 38.

35) Cf. Emil Brunner, *Justice and the Social Order* (New York: Harper & Brothers, 1945), pp. 271-72.

36) George A. Buttrick, *op. cit.,* p. 118.

37) John 7:17.

CHAPTER SEVEN   *The Good Earth and the Good Society*

1) Richard Niebuhr, *The Kingdom of God in America,* p. 193.

2) Arnold Toynbee, *A Study of History,* I Vol. abridgment (New York: Oxford University Press, 1946), p. 183.

3) F. J. E. Woodbridge, *The Son of Apollo,* pp. 81 ff.

4) Edward Bellamy, *Looking Backward* (Boston: Houghton Mifflin Company, 1898), pp. 167-69.

5) Cf. the account by James Dombrowski of the Christian Commonwealth Colony in Georgia in his *Early Days of Christian Socialism in America* (New York: Columbia University Press, 1936), chap. xii.

6) Karl Mannheim, *Ideology and Utopia* (New York: Harcourt, Brace and Company, 1936), p. 179.

7) *Ibid.,* pp. 217-26.

8) Quoted in W. C. Barclay, *Challenge and Power* (Nashville: Abingdon-Cokesbury Press, 1936), p. 61.

9) William E. Hocking, *Thoughts on Death and Life* (New York: Harper & Brothers, 1937), pp. 12-26.

10) Malvern Conference Report, *Malvern, 1941; the Life of the Church and the Order of Society* (London: Longmans, Green and Company, 1942).

11) David E. Lilienthal, *TVA—Democracy on the March* (New York: Harper & Brothers, 1944), pp. 83-84.

12) Fairfield Osborn, *Our Plundered Planet* (Boston: Little, Brown & Company, 1948); and William Vogt, *The Road to Survival* (New York: Wm. Sloane Associates, Inc., 1948).

13) R. B. Y. Scott and Gregory Vlastos, eds., *Towards the Christian Revolution* (New York: Harper & Brothers, 1936), p. 69.

14) Karl Barth, *Church and State,* p. 83.

15) Professor John Bennett pointed out at the Interseminary Conference at Oxford, Ohio, in June of 1947, the importance of historical development in making possible freedom in spite of Church establishment.

16) See *Dissenting Opinions of Mr. Justice Holmes,* arr. Alfred Lief (New York: The Vanguard Press, 1929), p. 9.

17) Elizabeth Hawes, "American Women Don't Get a Break," *Reader's Scope,* February, 1947, Vol. 4, No. 9.

18) Cf. William E. Hocking, *Freedom of the Press* (Chicago: University of Chicago Press, 1947).

19) Arnold Toynbee speaking on the University of Chicago Round Table, March 23, 1947, No. 470, Round Table Publications.

20) Herbert Spencer, *First Principles*, 4th ed. (New York: A. L. Burt Company, 1880); Oswald Spengler, *The Decline of the West* (New York: Alfred A. Knopf, 1926-28); Pitirim Sorokin, *The Crisis of Our Age* (New York: E. P. Dutton & Company, Inc., 1941). Sorokin is less deterministic than the others, especially in his latest book, *The Reconstruction of Humanity* (Boston: The Beacon Press, 1948).

21) Gunnar Myrdal, *An American Dilemma*, 2 vols. (New York: Harper & Brothers, 1944), pp. 1024, 1021.

22) Quincy Wright, *A Study of War* (Chicago: University of Chicago Press, 1942), pp. 6, 1223.

23) Wayne D. Williams, "What Instrumentality for the Administration of International Justice Will Most Effectively Promote the Establishment and Maintenance of International Law and Order?" *American Bar Association Journal*, September, 1944.

24) Quoted from a published sermon in *Faith at Work*, Vol. I, No. 2, October, 1945, published by the Religious Associates of the NCPAC.

CHAPTER EIGHT   *Growth in Grace: the Final Assurance*

1) Reinhold Niebuhr, *The Nature and Destiny of Man*, Vol. II, *passim*.

2) S. Kierkegaard, *Purity of Heart Is to Will One Thing*, trans. Douglas Steere (New York: Harper & Brothers, rev. ed., 1948).

3) Jacques Barzun, *Teacher in America*, p. 201.

4) Bernard of Clairvaux, *Loving God*, 15, 39 (Opera 1360).

5) Matthew 5:48. Moffatt translation.

6) W. E. Sangster, *The Path to Perfection* (Nashville: Abingdon-Cokesbury Press, 1943). Textual analysis in chap. iii.

7) R. Newton Flew, *The Idea of Perfection in Christian Theology* (London: Oxford University Press, 1934).

8) W. Norman Pittenger, "What the Church has to Give," *The Christian Century*, Vol. 62, No. 11, March 14, 1945, p. 333.

9) E. E. Aubrey, *Man's Search for Himself* (Nashville: Abingdon-Cokesbury Press, 1940), esp. chap. ii.

10) Quoted in Rollo May, *The Springs of Creative Living* (Nashville: Abingdon-Cokesbury Press, 1940), p. 47.

11) Olga Lengyel, *Five Chimneys* (Chicago: Ziff-Davis Publishing Company, 1947), p. 212.

12) Cf. A. N. Whitehead, *Process and Reality*, chap. i.

13) Gordon W. Allport, *Personality* (New York: Henry Holt and Company, Inc., 1937), p. 215.

14) A. N. Whitehead, *Science and the Modern World*, p. 26.

15) Daniel T. Jenkins, *The Nature of Catholicity* (London: Faber & Faber, Ltd., 1942), p. 65.

16) Professor H. N. Wieman has clarified the meaning of faith as commitment. Cf. *The Source of Human Good* (Chicago: University of Chicago Press, 1946), pp. 46-53.

17) Jonathan Edwards, *Works*, Vol. III, p. 45.

18) *Ibid.*, p. 48.

19) *Ibid.*, p. 34.

20) *Ibid.*, p. 63; cf. p. 202.

21) Quoted in William Manson, *Jesus the Messiah* (Philadelphia: Westminster Press, 1946), p. 62.

22) *Ibid.*, pp. 62-63.

23) William E. Hocking, *Human Nature and Its Remaking* (New Haven: Yale University Press, rev. ed., 1929), p. 411.

24) Douglas C. Macintosh, *Personal Religion* (New York: Charles Scribner's Sons, 1942), pp. 141-42.

25) Reinhold Niebuhr, *The Nature and Destiny of Man*, Vol. I, chap. vii.

26) I am indebted to Wilhelm Pauck for this definition.

27) John Calvin, *Institutes of the Christian Religion*, 7th American ed. (Philadelphia: Westminster Press, 1936), Vol. I, p. 291.

28) St. Augustine, commentary on Psalm CXLVII, sec. 12.

29) Calvin, *op. cit.*, p. 750.

30) A. D. Lindsay, *The Two Moralities*, quoted in Dorothy Sayers, *The Mind of the Maker* (New York: Harcourt, Brace and Company, Inc., 1941), p. 192.

31) Philippians 2:12-13.

32) I Thessalonians 3:12.

33) Colossians 3:9.

34) *The Westminster Confession*, chap. IX, secs. 4-5.

ADDITIONAL NOTES (1965)

Note 7 to Chapter Six is concerned with the position of the Roman Catholic Church on the relation of church and state. The discussion in the Second Vatican Council must now be included in any interpretation of that position. See *Council Speeches of Vatican II*, edited by Hans Küng, Yves Congar, and Daniel O'Hanlon. (Paulist Press, Glen Rock, New Jersey, 1964). Cf. John Courtney Murray, *We Hold These Truths: Catholic Reflections on the American Proposition*, (New York: Sheed and Ward, 1960).

Note 12 to Chapter Six can now include the more recent Roman Catholic discussion of birth control. See Stanislas de Lestapis, *Family Planning and Modern Problems: A Catholic Analysis*. (New York: Herder and Herder, 1961), and *Contraception and Holiness: The Catholic Predicament*, by Archbishop Thomas D. Roberts and others (New York: Herder and Herder, 1964).

INDEX